Walking as Mature Christians

Walking as Mature Christians

WALKING WITH JESUS
VOLUME FOUR

*An Expository Commentary
based upon Paul's Letter to the Ephesians*

(CHAPTER FOUR VERSES 1-16)

ROBERT B. CALLAHAN, SR.

RESOURCE *Publications* • Eugene, Oregon

WALKING AS MATURE CHRISTIANS
An Expository Commentary based upon Paul's Letter to the Ephesians
(Chapter 4 Verses 1-16)

Copyright © 2012 Robert B. Callahan, Sr. All rights reserved. Except for brief quotations in critical publications or reviews, no part of this book may be reproduced in any manner without prior written permission from the publisher. Write: Permissions, Wipf and Stock Publishers, 199 W. 8th Ave., Suite 3, Eugene, OR 97401.

Resource Publications
An Imprint of Wipf and Stock Publishers
199 W. 8th Ave., Suite 3
Eugene, OR 97401
www.wipfandstock.com

ISBN 13: 978-1-978-1-60899-648-3
Manufactured in the U.S.A.

All scripture quotations, unless otherwise indicated, are taken from the Holy Bible, The King James Study Bible, Copyright ©1983, 1988. (Previously published as the Liberty Annotated Study Bible and as The Annotated Study Bible, King James Version) Copyright © 1988 by Liberty University. Thomas Nelson Publishers.

*For my wife, Ginger,
whose encouragement, faith,
love, and objectivity contributed
significantly to Walking With Jesus*

Topical Categories in Walking with Jesus
(An Expository Commentary)

Volume One	Volume Two	Volume Three	Volume Four
The Triune God Speaks to the Saints	*Sin and Redemption*	*Christ's Prisoner*	*Walking As Mature Christians*
To the Faithful in Christ Jesus	Sin and God's Wrath	For This Cause— God's Glory	Living in Harmony With Christ
God's Will— Spiritual Blessings	God, Rich in Mercy and Grace	Revealing God's Hidden Truths	Unity in the Triune God The Holy Spirit
Trusting in Him	A Right Relationship With God	Praying to the Father	The Lord Jesus Christ
Praying for Christians	Reconciliation	Believing God's Power	God, the Father
	Praying Through the Holy Spirit		Grace According to Christ's Gifts
	God's Foundation (Apostles and Prophets)		Maturing in Christ

Topical Categories in Walking with Jesus

(An Expository Commentary)

Volume Five	Volume Six	Volume Seven	Volume Eight
Following Christ	*Walking Wisely*	*Satan and God's Armor*	*Christ's Ambassadors*
Alienated from God	Christ-Like Conduct	Family Relationships	A Call to Discipleship
Ye Have Not So Learned Christ	No Inheritance in the Kingdom of God and Christ	Life's Basic Relationship	Wearing God's Armor
Christ-Like Conduct	Walking in the Light	The Whole Armor of God	Christ's Ambassadors
	Walking Circumspectly	Satan and His Evil Forces	
	The Marriage Relationship		
	Christ and His Church		

Ephesians "brings one into an atmosphere of unbounded spiritual affluence that creates within one's heart deepest peace and assurance. It is impossible to live habitually in Ephesians and be depressed."

RUTH PAXSON

Contents

Volume Four: Topical Categories xi
Foreword xiii
Preface xv
Acknowledgments xvii
The Question of Authorship xix
Introduction xxi

1 Prisoner of the Lord 1

2 Regeneration 10

3 Called to Walk in His Footsteps 17

4 Unity 28

5 One Body, and One Spirit 34

6 The Person of the Holy Spirit 43

7 The Holy Spirit 51

8 Looking Forward 64

9 King of Kings, Lord of Lords 73

10 Thy Blood Shed for Me 82

11 Baptism 90

12 God the Father 98

13 But Unto Every One 106

14 Worship Intelligently 114

15 Faith and Knowledge 122

16 The Perfect Man 131

17 Henceforth 137

18 Cunning Craftiness 146

19 Growing Up Into Christ 154

20 Weaned From Milk 165

21 Spirit Producing Fruit 173

Outline Questions 183
Bibliography 227
Scripture Index 229

Volume Four: Topical Categories

Category	Scripture	Chapters
Living in Harmony With Christ	Eph. 4:1–3	1–4
Unity in the Triune God	Eph 4:4–6	5–12
(The Holy Spirit)		(5–8)
(The Lord Jesus Christ)		(9–11)
(God, the Father)		(12)
Grace According to Christ's Gifts	Eph 4:7–13	13–16
Maturing in Christ	Eph 4:14–16	17–21

Foreword

Robert Callahan's multi-volume work of Paul's Letter to the Ephesians is both a welcomed and long-overdue guide for Christian living today. The Apostle's sense of the eternity and greatness of God, his emphasis on the living reality and exaltation of Christ, his devotion to God's grace as an unearned gift of enduring love, and his call to an ardent and faithful discipleship all witness to an urgency and renewal critically needed in our time. Callahan's heart and style rise to meet this challenge and to convey God's message of hope and promise, of presence and courage, to Christian souls of any and every contemporary Christian tradition.

Callahan's format allows for both a devotional and studious usage. One can permit one's soul to savor every spiritual nuance the author uncovers, verse by verse, mark the passage, and return later for further nourishment. Or one can linger from text to text, gleaning with the author both theological and spiritual insight for enhancing personal discipleship, equally applicable in the arena of church and society.

The author draws on an array of insightful theological and spiritual wisdom, garnered from scholars and saints alike, theologians and missionaries. Calvin's Institutes guide Callahan's expositions, as well as the work of Markus Barth – known for his commentary on Ephesians and his delineation of Pauline theology. The author cites frequent and astute observations from Barth's exegesis of this nature. In addition, Callahan makes wise usage of Martyn Lloyd-Jones' emphasis on "experiencing the living Christ." For Lloyd-Jones, as well as the author, mere intellectual knowledge of the Christ fails to undergird one's faith or discipleship, when life's journey truly becomes sore bestead. Callahan also draws from the great 17th century theologian William Gurnall's delightful work: The Christian in Complete Armour. Perhaps students of Church history remember how both John Newton and Charles Spurgeon prized Gurnall's approach and piety and preferred it to many perspicacious studies available in their time. Gurnall's Complete Armour is known for its pithy, fervent, and wise counsel that confronts human vagaries with the truth about the self. In that respect, so too does Robert Callahan's gentle but firm counsel enrich the Christian heart and inspire one to a higher level of discipleship. No one can fail to sense this in Walking With Jesus. Whether encouraged to venture this methodology owing to his own years as a Presbyterian elder, or as an avid member and participant of the bi-annual Calvin's Colloquiums for the past 30 years, or as a fond reader of Ruth Paxson's The Wealth, Walk and Warfare of the Christian, the result is the same: a powerful, inspirational, and theologically heart-warming guide to discipleship today.

Ministers, Christian educators, seminary students, laypersons, and lovers of Jesus' life will find Callahan's work immensely valuable. His volumes deserve our grateful and sincere attention, as we too seek to walk with Jesus.

Benjamin W. Farley
Younts Professor Emeritus of Bible, Religion, and Philosophy
Erskine College, Due West, South Carolina

Preface

Paul's Epistle to the Ephesians shows us the joy and challenge of being united to Christ in his death and resurrection. It takes us from being seated with Him in the heavenlies (chapter 2), down to the battles we must wage, in His armor, with powers of evil (Eph. 6). In a balanced and judicious manner, longtime Presbyterian elder, Bob Callahan, exercises remarkable insight in opening to believers the vital truths of Ephesians; truths that once taken in, transform the attitude towards life, and often set the soul singing!

As a professor of theology, I have carefully worked through one of his multivolumed series, and found it to be theologically sound: evangelical and scholarly at the same time. It has spiritual depth and is extremely practical; it is accessible in good, clear English. It is neither a commentary, nor a series of sermons. In some ways it reminds me of some of the ancient Patristic engagements with a series of texts of Holy Scripture. It brings the reader into the presence of the Most High, and – if considered thoughtfully and prayerfully, is likely to cause him to sit down under the canopy of God's love.

The journey of Christians in today's world is very demanding indeed, and Bob's work is intended to be a guide to help every pilgrim 'Walking with Jesus.' It will be a rich resource for Sunday Schools, Bible studies, as well as for individual devotions.

Douglas F. Kelly
Reformed Theological Seminary
Charlotte, NC

Acknowledgments

The crafting of Walking With Jesus was not a "one man show" but numerous people working together to present a formidable work. Three guiding lights have been paramount in the minds of those making significant contributions: one, presenting the theology in accord with the tenets of the Reformed Faith; two, employing language that presents the Gospel in a meaningful and understandable light; and, three, expounding upon Scripture in a clear, concise, and forthright manner.

It has been God's blessing that the following ministers and theologians have enthusiastically and willingly provided their time and talents to enhance this work. They are:

Dr. Frank Barker, Founder and Pastor Emeritus of the Briarwood Presbyterian Church, Birmingham, AL

Dr. Benjamin W. Farley, Younts Professor Emeritus, Bible, Religion, and Philosophy, Erskine College, Due West, SC

Dr. James C. Goodloe, IV, Executive Director, Foundation for Reformed Theology, Richmond, VA

Dr. Todd Jones, Senior Minister, First Presbyterian Church, Nashville, TN

Dr. Douglas Kelly, Richard Jordan, Professor of Theology, Reformed Theological Seminary, Charlotte, NC

Dr. Norman McCrummen, Senior Pastor, Spring Hill Presbyterian Church, Mobile, AL

Dr. Mark Mueller, Senior Pastor, First Presbyterian Church, Huntsville, AL

Dr. Richard Ray, Former Managing Director of John Knox Press, Montreat, NC

Without the knowledge, wisdom, and encouragement of these individuals this work would neither have become a reality nor available to individuals seeking a better understanding of the teachings of the Scripture and the joy of walking daily with the Lord Jesus.

Several others have labored diligently to create this work, and to produce the finished product. Our daughter, Karen Callahan Myrick, made significant contributions during the drafting process through her knowledge of grammar. Ms. Lynn Sledge, as the copy editor, judiciously reviewed the manuscript and made valuable contributions for improving it. Four ladies, Helen Marshall, D'Anne Dendy, Kelly Comferford, and Elizabeth Annan, worked tirelessly, with dedication, to prepare draft after draft and to make positive contributions to the project. In addition, Wick Skinner made invaluable contributions through his attention to details, grammar, and vocabulary.

It is not possible to thank them sufficiently for their dedication to making this volume a desirable repository of Christian truths, and in so doing to cheerfully work on draft after draft, to recommend enhancements, and to make appropriate changes in the text. Their unselfish contributions are too many to enumerate. May God bless them.

The Question of Authorship

Recent scholars have questioned the authorship of the letter to the Ephesians and have been less convinced that it was the Apostle Paul. However, for the sake of simplicity of expression we will abide by the traditional view and refer to Paul as its author.

Introduction

The creation of this work was the result of unusual developments which some would attribute to happenstance and others to God's providence. You may be the judge after considering the following.

During May 2000 a friend invited my wife and me to visit the Spring Hill Presbyterian Church in Mobile and hear their new minister, Norman McCrummen. We accepted his invitation.

The following March, Dr. McCrummen was preaching on anything but Ephesians when he interrupted his sermon, paused long enough to slowly scan the congregation twice, and said, "I want everyone to read the first and second chapters of Ephesians by next Sunday" and promptly returned to his sermon. The next day I called him and said, "I can't do it" a few times. Finally, his light went on and he said, "What can't you do?" I said, "I can't read the first and second chapters of Ephesians by next Sunday." He asked, "Why can't you? It will only take ten to fifteen minutes." I responded, "I have fifty-eight to sixty expository messages on the first two chapters of Ephesians that took thirty to thirty-five minutes to present." His response was, "I want to read all those and everything else you have on Ephesians." Thus began the long, arduous, and heart-warming journey of converting handwritten notes along with printed ones into the written word. It has been a joyful, though demanding experience.

Paul's Letter to the Ephesians has been described as "The holiest of the holies." My love affair with it began in the 1980's when I read a book containing great sermons of the twentieth century. The most impressive one was written by Martyn Lloyd-Jones. As a result, I read other works of his including his exposition of Ephesians. Thereafter, unexpectedly, I was asked to teach an adult Bible Study Group. They said they would provide the material, but I demurred and said, "I would gather my own material." This set in motion the process of acquiring knowledge through the best expository works available at the time on Ephesians including Martyn

Lloyd-Jones, William Gurnall, Ruth Paxson, Markus Barth, John Calvin, Otto Weber, and others.

The objective was to present the essence of Paul's letter as it was presented to him by the Lord Jesus and the Holy Spirit. Further, to mine the gold available in the fruitful works of those fertile minds that God had cultivated and enabled to expound upon the truths that His only begotten Son had revealed to His apostles and disciples. Therefore, it was a paramount obligation to express God's truths in a simple, straightforward manner according to the dictates of the Holy Spirit so that the reader may grasp it and interpret it according to the will of our Lord and Saviour Jesus Christ.

The need for the truths of the Gospel is as great today as it was in the first century. The conditions are similar and the challenges facing our culture reveal the need for knowing the living God and His Son. Today, the people of faith require the same spiritual nourishment as those brave souls of the early days after the Resurrection, who would rather face death than deny their Lord and Saviour.

There are people in responsible positions in Christ's church who deny Him by: their passivity; seeking secular acceptance; and failing to honor Him in public. These apostasies negatively impact members of organized Christian churches as well as non-believers.

They create an environment in which unrighteousness flourishes. This results in irreverence as aptly described by R.W. Dale, "Where there is irreverence for the divine law the vision of God becomes fainter; as the vision of God becomes fainter the restraints of the Divine Righteousness are lessened and at last the vision of God is lost altogether." May God enlighten us regarding His infallible Word so that we will hunger and thirst for righteousness, and for the vision of God to shine brighter and brighter as we serve Him with courage, wisdom, justice, and self-control.

This expository commentary is designed to bring individuals, whether they are spiritually children, adolescents or adults into a closer, more mature relationship with the Lord Jesus Christ. It begins with the Triune God; presents the doctrines of the Christian faith; reminds us "that we henceforth be no more children, tossed to and fro . . . but speaking the truth in love, may grow up into Him in all things, . . . even Christ." It continues by emphasizing the importance of being renewed in the spirit of your mind; putting on the new man, which after God is created in righteousness and true holiness; using the whole armor of God to thwart the manifold attacks of Satan; and concluding with the admonition to conduct ourselves as Christ's ambassadors.

The spiritual food contained ranges from milk and honey to tough meat. The flavor of this exposition encompasses all varieties—sweet, sour, pleasant, bitter, tart, tasteless, dry, burned, and succulent. Do not reject the nourishment because of its texture or flavor, but seek to understand it despite your preferences, since it provides food for good health and strength for joyful living. May God's truths flourish in your heart and mind, and enable you to withstand the tests, trials, and tribulations that come your way as you are "Walking With Jesus."

In presenting this work, I realize everyone has different challenges. The fascinating part of God's Word is that it meets us where we are. The question is, will we meet Him there, hear what He has to say, and accept the nourishment He offers?

The words of William Gurnall are appropriate and enlightening in contemplating God's Word. He said prior to expounding upon Ephesians, "The fare that I shall be serving during the coming weeks will be from God's own table. If perchance it does not go down well or should not have the flavor that you desire, please do not despise the provider of the food, but blame the cook who has prepared it and is serving it." To that I say, Amen!

The courses being served by this cook are described herein. May they provide the taste and nourishment you are seeking.

Robert B. Callahan, Sr.

1

Prisoner of the Lord

I THEREFORE, the prisoner of (in) *the Lord, beseech you that ye walk worthy of the vocation* (calling) *wherewith ye are called,*
　With all lowliness and meekness (gentleness), *with long suffering, forbearing* (bearing with) *one another in love;*
　Endeavoring to keep the unity of the Spirit in the bond of peace [Eph. 4:1–3].

God has blessed us mightily with His Word, His Son Christ Jesus, and through the revealing power and illumination of the Holy Spirit. The first three chapters of this magnificent letter have revealed God's purpose, God's way of reconciliation, the unsearchable riches of Christ, the eternal purpose which God purposed in Christ Jesus, and Paul's beautiful, revealing prayer in the last eight verses of the third chapter.

Much time has been spent considering doctrine and examining it in light of the basic truths contained in both the Old Testament and the New Testament. The first three chapters reveal that God's wealth, power, and love are available to us and will work within us.

The wealth bestowed upon us is not to be hoarded, but it is to be circulated so it can minister to others. The revelation of the divine truths becomes fruitful only as it is transmitted into the actual living experience. The wealth bestowed upon the person *in Christ* should manifest itself in his or her life.

The better we know God's truths and believe them, then the greater responsibility we have to live accordingly. Our thoughts regarding God's knowledge and belief become so intertwined that God's truths express themselves positively as we continue walking with Him.

"The first three chapters tell us how God sees us in Christ in the heavenlies, while four through six tell us how men should see Christ in us on earth," according to the remarkable Ruth Paxson. These three chapters should bring us closer and closer to Jesus Christ and strengthen us so that we can follow Him more closely. Paul communicates to the Ephesians in a practical manner what is revealed in and through Jesus Christ.

It is not to be considered from a distance, but to become part of our mind, body, soul, and spirit. It is to become the standard for our daily living. How can it become the standard if we do not know the details, if we do not rehearse and practice, and if we do not covenant?

How can a cook prepare a fine meal with excellent dishes if he or she does not follow the recipes, select the proper ingredients, devote the time and energy, and concentrate?

Why do we expect the important issues of life to fall easily into place, or to cost us nothing, when considering for even a moment that Jesus Christ went to the Cross, was crucified, suffered, and died for each of us, individually? We have a responsibility to learn more and more.

The first three chapters have been entirely doctrinal. The Apostle has been presenting the great doctrines of the faith and explaining the essential points to understanding the way of salvation. Having done this, Paul proceeds to the practical application of doctrine. He describes in the remaining chapters how doctrine is related to daily living. So, at this juncture of Paul's letter, we are at a real division. We are at a transition point. However, we must keep our feet on the ground and be aware of certain factors.

The word *therefore* introduces Chapter 4 and signals a transition, but the Apostle Paul returns to doctrine in the fourth verse. He does not deal in absolute divisions, because he could not. We also cannot separate doctrine and practice. People who think we can miss much of the glory of faith in Christ Jesus.

When Paul used the word *therefore* he made a definite, clear connection between faith and practice. First the doctrine, then the application: the two go together. In the first three verses of Chapter 4, Paul deals with application, then he goes back to doctrine, saying,

> *There is one body, and one Spirit, even as ye are called in one hope of your calling;*
> *One Lord, one faith, one baptism,*
> *One God and Father of all, who is above all, and through all, and in you all* [Eph. 4:4–6].

The two are intertwined. They cannot and should not be separated. Then, Paul goes back to application during portions of the fourth, fifth, and sixth chapters. Yet he will also present doctrine.

The first thing the Apostle does, after shifting the emphasis from doctrine to the practical application of it, is to urge the Ephesians (and us) to *walk worthy of the vocation* (calling) *wherewith ye are called, . . .* The Greek word for calling is *klēsis*. It is revealing because it "is always used in the New Testament of that calling the origin, nature and destiny of which are heavenly." This is no ordinary calling, nor a temporary one, but a calling for life. Notice when Paul says this. It is immediately after a prayer wherein he prays . . . *that ye might be filled with all the fullness of God. Now unto him that is able to do exceeding abundantly above all that we ask, or think, according to the power that worketh in us, . . .* [Eph. 3:19–20].

Why does Paul use the word *walk*? Ruth Paxson states that "to walk implies purpose, starting for a goal; progress, steadily advancing step by step; perseverance, keeping on until the goal is reached. Walking stands for steady, sustained motion, and involves the action of the mind in the decision to start; of the heart in the desire to continue, and of the will in the determination to arrive.

"Such a walk requires on the manward side fullest cooperation with God. It demands a set purpose, a steady progress, and a strong perseverance. The Christian must resolutely purpose to "put off the old man," and to "put on the new man"; he must keep steadily on his course without faltering or fainting in spite of all opposition by not "giving place to the devil," or "grieving the spirit," but rather by being filled with the spirit and empowered by Him.

"But how exceedingly, difficult is such a walk! The old habits of life are so binding, the worldly currents about us are so strong; the temptations of the world, the flesh, and the devil are so subtle; the fear of being considered peculiar is so gripping; the opportunity of fellowship with spiritually-minded Christians is so limited. To maintain a steady, sustained consistency in daily conduct is not an easy task. It is far easier to float downstream with the tide of nominal Christianity; to drift in the listlessness and lukewarmness of a worldly church; to creep along as a spiritual babe, fed on the milk of elementary doctrines of salvation; easier even to mount up with eagles wings and soar to spiritual heights of sudden inspiration on some spiritual Mount of Transfiguration only to relapse into a backslidden condition when facing the stern realities of Christian living in an unsympathetic atmosphere; very much easier, even, to run rising to some particular task such as teaching a Bible class, or leading a meeting, or preaching a sermon, than to practice consistently in the home, office, or social circle the truth preached. A daily consistent Christlike walk; no stagnancy, slump or sloth—how hard!" Yes, it is hard, but by the grace of God, the presence of the risen Christ and the power of the Holy Spirit we can *walk worthy of the vocation* (calling) *wherewith ye are called.*

Paul begins this section saying,

> I THEREFORE, *the prisoner of* (in) *the Lord, beseech you that ye walk worthy of the vocation* (calling) *wherewith ye are called,* . . . [Eph. 4:1].

The Greek word for *therefore* means "then, now." Paul says because of what has happened, because of what has been presented, *then* or *now* I beseech you.

Therefore, in this instance, does not indicate beginning something new, but conveys the meaning that what follows is a continuation of what has gone before. There is not a change of thought, but there is a specific call to *walk worthy*. The position of the Christian, the person *in Christ*, is to be in harmony with Christ in his or her daily living. Being *in Christ* should result in growing up into Christ.

Before proceeding with the initial verses of the fourth chapter, there are certain observations to consider. First, there is a distinct difference between the lofty, powerful prayer at the end of the third chapter and the initial verses of the fourth chapter. Consider Paul prays,

- *That he would grant you, according to the riches of His glory,*
- *Strengthened with might by his Spirit in the inner man;*
- *That Christ may dwell in your hearts by faith;*
- *That ye, being rooted and grounded in love,*
- *May be able to comprehend* (understand) *with all saints what is the breadth* (width), *and length, and depth, and height;*
- *To know the love of Christ, which passeth knowledge,*
- *That ye might be filled with all the fullness of God.*
- *According to the power that worketh in us,*

   [Selections from Eph. 3:16–20].

Paul follows this uplifting prayer to God the Father beseeching Him to bless His chosen ones with incomparable blessings by directing *the saints which are at Ephesus, and . . . faithful in Christ Jesus: . . .* (including you and me) that they are to walk according to Christ's dictates, not their own standards.

- *Walk worthy of the vocation* (calling) *wherewith ye are called,*
- *With all lowliness and meekness* (gentleness),
- *With long-suffering,*
- *Forbearing* (bearing with) *one another in love;*
- *Endeavoring to keep the unity of the Spirit in the bond of peace*

[Selections from Eph. 4:1–3].

It is characteristic of Paul to connect faith and righteousness, and then to identify the human responsibilities based upon divine revelations and love. One thing about Paul, he will wake us up, and he will shake us out of our lethargy, if we will listen to God's will revealed through his writings.

We are to *walk worthy . . . With all lowliness and meekness* (gentleness), *with long-suffering, Forbearing* (Bearing with) *one another in love*. Chances are we would not have described our walk in the same terms, but would have wanted to elevate ourselves and attain a higher or more exalted position.

Instead of urging us to perform mighty tasks or appealing to our egos, Paul exhorts us to humility, meekness, and long-suffering. This passage, and how it is explicitly stated, should send us an important message. Often times we begin with God, but too soon we lose sight of Him and our dependence upon Him. Therefore, we become occupied with our own dreams, and the power, glory, and honor that might be ours.

A nineteenth century minister and expositor of the scriptures, R.W. Dale, stated it succinctly,

> "Religious excitement originating by direct contact with God will always enlarge and exalt our conception of God's greatness, and will deepen our sense of dependence on Him . . . , but as emotion becomes more intense and as our conceptions of the Christian life become more and more glorious, the infinite greatness of God's righteousness and power and grace will inspire us with deeper wonder and awe."

Then he goes on to say,

> "On the other hand, religious excitement created by the imagination, though it may suggest lofty ideas of moral and spiritual perfection, and inspire a vehement and chivalrous desire to translate these ideas into conduct, will leave us with a new sense of our own greatness rather than a new sense of the greatness of God."

What a beautiful yet practical thought.

Please note Paul puts humility first. Why would he do that? Think, if you will: Christ himself was lowly in heart; He descended from the heights; He took the form of a servant; and He came not to do His own will, but the will of His Father.

The doctrine, the dignity, the glory, and the power contained in the first three chapters are immediately followed by Paul exhorting us to humility and harmony in our life in the Spirit. We have received the unsearchable riches, the immeasurable blessings we are able to share with Christ, and we are *in Christ* where God's grace and wealth have been conferred upon us. We have received abundantly; it has been given to us. *It has all come from God, nothing from us. Note, nothing comes from us.*

How does one receive humility? "Lowliness and humility are realized by: prayer; communion with God; meditating upon God's righteousness; considering our own sin; contemplating God's greatness and our limitations; God's fullness, our dependence; and God's blessings through Christ," according to the incomparable John Calvin.

Calvin, in his exposition of this Scripture, says, "Paul put humility first because it is the first step if we are to attain unity. Humility produces meekness which makes us patient, and by bearing with our brethren we keep that unity which would be broken a hundred times a day." Let us remember that in cultivating brotherly kindness we must begin with humility.

Whence come impudence, pride, and insult towards the brethren? Whence come quarrels, taunts, and reproaches, except from everyone loving himself too much and pleasing himself too much?

These are practical thoughts to consider as we examine the latter portion of Paul's letter. We are to rid ourselves of certain thoughts and ideas if we are to acquire and exhibit meekness. Whoever receives this gift will overlook and tolerate many things that occur due to the actions or comments of others. It is fruitless to direct or command one to be patient unless we can tame his or her mind. You cannot speak of meekness unless you begin with humility.

Meekness is the absence of the disposition to assert personal rights, either in the presence of God or of men. Meekness finds no reason for distrusting God, His righteousness, or His goodness. Meekness is not conscious of suffering any injustice. It has no personal claims to defend; it is slow to resent insult and injury. If it does, it will see it as a violation against God and His laws, not against the individual. Meekness is not eager for great honors, position, or recognition.

Therefore, if they are withheld there will not be any bitterness or animosity. Where there is meekness, there will be long-suffering.

Paul spent much time praying for those who are *in Christ* regarding their conduct, daily actions, and reactions to events and people. Paul was realistic, and so should we be. He did not assume that all those who are loyal to Christ will be able to keep His Commandments perfectly. Nor did he assume that all those who are *in Christ* have eliminated and overcome all the basic elements and passions of human nature.

He recognized that both the people who are not *in Christ* and those who are will do the following: treat others unjustly; judge others ignorantly and not very generously; be inconsiderate and discourteous; say ugly things about others; be selfish and wayward; exhibit arrogance, ambition, impatience, perversity; and be greedy and self-centered. Christ bears with these imperfections. He is willing to forgive when a person sincerely seeks forgiveness. He is willing to impart His power and strength.

What is Paul doing in the last half of this Epistle? He is appealing to the Ephesians to practice what he has been proclaiming. He describes what should be the result of understanding the great doctrines of the Christian faith.

When embarking upon this fourth chapter, it may be well to ask:

- What is your reaction to applying doctrine in a practical manner?
- Do you think the remaining three chapters may be anticlimactic?
- Would you have preferred concluding our study of Ephesians at the end of the third chapter?

We must continue; we cannot stop. We must acquire knowledge about applying doctrine. As we do, there are certain factors to identify and remember: The word *therefore* should help us learn how to read Scripture. We not only need to learn how to read Scripture, but we need to remind ourselves about this important resource.

We are *not* to pick and choose as we read Scripture. We are to read all the scriptures, every part of them. We are to read it from Genesis to Revelation. We are to understand the significance of each portion and how it is all interrelated. We are to grasp the meaning of it all. There is a balance in Scripture, and the context of each verse, paragraph, or section is important.

People have a tendency to take portions of Scripture out of context. Some want to formulate a doctrine by using only a portion of Scripture. The word *therefore* reminds us of the wholeness of Scripture. It emphasizes the importance of connectivity and the relationship of one portion to another. It points us in the direction we are to go and how we are to live.

Unfortunately, there is always the danger of forgetting that being *in Christ* is a way of life, and it is to be exhibited in daily living. While some people regard Christianity as a system of morality and ethics, others want to emphasize doctrine or works. Others get caught up in certain facets and completely miss what God is trying to give them or how He wants them to act.

Although doctrine comes first, we cannot stop there. We must go to its application. Conversely we cannot just consider experiences and ignore doctrine. A balance is not only desired, but is required between doctrine and experience. Paul wrote to Titus, saying,

> *For the grace of God that bringeth salvation hath appeared to all men,*
> *Teaching us that, denying ungodliness and worldly lusts, we should live soberly, righteously, and godly, in this present world (age);*
> *Looking for that blessed hope, and the glorious appearing of the great God and our Saviour Jesus Christ;*
> *Who gave himself for us, that he might redeem us from all iniquity, and purify unto himself a peculiar* (his own special) *people, zealous of good works* [Titus 2:11–14].

To know doctrine is important. To have experiences is important.

Calvin provides additional light as we continue Walking With Jesus. He focuses our minds by proclaiming that "the revelation of God's grace necessarily brings with it exhortations to a godly life."

He then proceeds to amplify upon Paul's words *"denying ungodliness.* He now lays down the rule by which we may order our lives well, and tells us that we ought to begin by renouncing our former way of life, two features of which he mentions—*ungodliness and worldly lusts.* Under ungodliness I include not only the superstitions in which they had erred, but the irreligious neglect of God that prevails among men until they have been enlightened into the knowledge of the truth. For although they make some profession of religion, they never fear and reverence God sincerely from the heart, but rather have slumbering consciences, so that nothing is further from their thoughts than their duty to serve God ... Meditation on the heavenly life begins after regeneration; before that our desires are directed to the world and cling to it.

"Who gave Himself for us . . . . Christ offered Himself for us that He might redeem us from slavery to sin and purchase us for Himself as His possession. His grace necessarily brings with it newness of life, for those who go on serving sin make void the blessing of redemption. But now we are rescued from the bondage of sin that we may serve God's righteousness.

"From this he immediately passes to the second point about *a people for his own possession, zealous of good works,* by which he means that the fruit of redemption is lost to us, if we still held fast in the net of the world's sinful desires. To express more clearly, the fact that we have been consecrated to good works by the death of Christ, he uses the word purify, for it would be unworthy for us to let ourselves be polluted by the very stains that by His death God's Son has purged from us."

Some people think it would be nice to live in isolation. Other people would not be exposed to Christ, or know about Him, unless they see or hear it from us in our daily lives. That is awesome! Whether we realize it or not, every day we are to show what we know, what we have, and above all, Him in whom we believe. The life we live always results from either applying His teachings or not applying them.

The word *therefore* makes it perfectly clear that we are to engage in practical living. It tells us about the nature and character of the life we are to live. That conduct is determined by doctrine and results from applying it or failing to do so.

The sequence is always the same. Doctrine first, then its application. The order is never reversed. We are to act only when we are clear about God's doctrine, as it is revealed in Christ Jesus.

Amen!

2

Regeneration

And every man that hath this hope in him purifieth himself, even as he is pure.
Whosoever committeth sin transgresseth (commits lawlessness) *also the law: for sin is the transgression* (lawlessness) *of the law.*
And ye know that he was manifested to take away our sins; and in him is no sin [1 John 3:3–5].

Possibly a question or thought in the back of your mind as we discuss doctrine and its practical application is *sanctification*. Many of us are interested in sanctification, because it applies to self. Do you know how many times it appears in the New Testament? Five times, only five times. What does the word mean? The Greek word is *hagiasmos* and it means "separation" or "a setting apart."

The word *sanctified* appears in both the Old Testament and the New Testament thirty times. Also, *sanctify* appears numerous times in the Old Testament and the New Testament. In all instances it means "to separate" or "to set apart."

The first three chapters of Ephesians, with all their magnificent teaching, do not consider the Doctrine of Sanctification.

To know the love of Christ is not sanctification, to be filled with the fullness of God is not sanctification, and to be sealed with the Spirit is not sanctification. These things promote, encourage, and motivate sanctification, but they are not sanctification. The term or the words imply the making of something. It is a process that is being completed, it is incomplete, it is not a finished product. It means to make holy or the process of becoming holy.

You may recall the Greek word for *holy* used in the New Testament is *hagios*. It means "separate, set apart." Paul uses this word four times in his letter to the Ephesians in referring to:

> those who are chosen, . . . *that we should be holy and without blame before him (Christ) in love* [Eph. 1:4];

> *those who are in the building where Christ is the chief cornerstone and it . . . groweth unto a holy temple in the Lord* [Eph. 2:21];

> *the knowledge of Christ, . . . as it is now revealed unto his holy apostles and prophets by the Spirit;* . . . [Eph. 3:5]; and

> the church itself, . . . *that it should be holy and without blemish* [Eph. 5:27].

Paul speaks to us as God's chosen ones through Christ and tells us what we are to become and how we are to act.

Before considering the details of sanctification, there are certain thoughts to examine. It may be well to briefly address justification and sanctification, if that is possible. However, an examination is required in order to achieve a better understanding of the material in chapters four, five, and six.

"The doctrine of justification describes God's reconciling work in Jesus Christ as the act through which man, in himself unrighteous, is truly brought into harmony with God, and not just in name only," according to the esteemed theologian Otto Weber. We have been discussing God's covenant with man and that God is true to His covenant.

God Himself speaks *in Christ* and assures man, who has broken the covenant, of His own righteousness and loyalty to His covenant. This is the core of the Christian message *in Christ*. This is the theology of the Gospel of Christ. Jesus Christ is God's assurance that all our sins, little or great, have been forgiven. This truth has never been contested, although it has been distorted, embellished, and weakened.

It is important to remember that Jesus Christ "is also God's mighty claim upon our whole life," as stated in the Theological Declaration of Barmen. It is not that God is to satisfy only our longing for salvation, to fill in gaps, and to answer questions. When God justifies, He makes us right in our earthly, mortal life and reveals Himself as our Lord.

Justification does not contain everything that God's assurance makes available to us, and His "claim" upon us is more than what we call "sanctification."

However, in Jesus Christ we are justified and sanctified, accepted by God.

> *All scripture is given by inspiration of God, and is profitable for doctrine, for reproof, for correction, for instruction in righteousness:*
> *That the man of God may be perfect, thoroughly furnished* (equipped) *unto all good works* [2 Tim. 3:16–17].

It is *in Christ* that we become the people of God and are effectively claimed by Him. Our righteousness is outside ourselves. Thus we are not our own, we are the Lord's.

The question of justification and sanctification is not an easy or simple one. There are many misunderstandings and misconceptions in these areas. People want to discuss the relationship of "sanctification" to "justification." The New Testament does not combine these two doctrines, nor the discussion of them."

Paul developed the concept of the Doctrine of Justification. The term "sanctification" is noted throughout the New Testament. It has nuances and other terms, which are directed toward the same goal, such as "conversion," "regeneration," "renewal," and "good works." We need to remember that these terms describe a relationship to God, a relationship established *in Christ*. It is a relationship grasped and comprehended by both the individual and the community of believers. It is expressed in a number of different ways.

Older theology did not emphasize the concept of sanctification in proportion to its appearance in the New Testament. It is found occasionally among the older theologians. According to Weber, "it is found most strongly in Calvin," who at times has been described as the "theologian of sanctification." However, in Calvin's Institutes, sanctification is not the theme of one of his chapters. But he does write about "regeneration" and "repentance."

In other places terms like "renewal," "new life," "regeneration," and "conversion" are used instead of "sanctification." Why?

One group, Scholasticism, conceives of "sanctification" as part of justification. Therefore, it did not deal with it in a special way. Consequently, the Reformation did not have any special terminology to accept and embrace sanctification. However, there was a group, the

Nominalist, that developed and emphasized "meritorious works" or works of satisfaction. These became established and accepted in areas of the church at that time.

As a consequence many reformers treated or considered the substance of sanctification along the same lines as when they discussed "good works." This tendency resulted in "good works" becoming a problem or concern to the Reformation leaders.

It was very easy then, just as it is today, for the idea to grow and be accepted that good works should either take place with or be the result of justification. The result of all this was that good works were viewed as being damaging, useful, or necessary for salvation, which just about covers the waterfront. Ascribing this to justification resulted in the view that God's justifying act did not take into account man's sin, but did regard Christ's merit and grace.

Further, God's justifying judgment had eradicated man's sin and his past, but had imposed upon him the question of how he was going to spend the rest of his earthly life. This process of reasoning led to expanding the problem of "good works" into the question of "renewal," "regeneration," "conversion," and the "life of being a Christian." What was behind this? There was a sense of pastoral responsibility, and certainly there were some bitter experiences.

The emphasis placed by some of the Reformers on "by faith alone" produced the reaction or thinking that "regeneration," "the Christian life," or "conversion" were not important. This is certainly contra to New Testament theology.

The teaching "by faith alone" made people careless, or profane, or satisfied, or complacent. This resulted in many Reformers seldom expressing or giving appropriate consideration to sanctification according to the witness provided by Scripture. Calvin was an exception to this notable omission.

Most Reformers dealt with sanctification after discussing justification. This resulted in the interpretation or understanding that good works were a temporal consequence of justification.

Broadly speaking, the Reformation was satisfied with asserting that good works are the fruit of justification. Therefore, certain conclusions can be stated:

> one, Calvin does not place sanctification at the center of his thoughts or writings; and,

two, there were those who placed great emphasis on good works, producing their rejection of "merits" and affirming the idea of the "fruit of justification," which resulted in developing material for the Doctrine of Sanctification.

The relationship between justification and sanctification was seen primarily in the Reformation in terms of good works. However, there are not any Evangelical documents that speak of the necessity of good works in order to attain justification. Further, none of them implies that a justified person can be without good works.

What does the New Testament say? No one becomes righteous by the works of the law. The New Testament makes it very clear that God's impact upon a person is to have him or her produce good works, or as may be preferred living in harmony with the will of God. The New Testament teaches specifically about a person becoming a new creature. Paul says to the Corinthians,

> *If any man be in Christ, he is a new creature: old things are passed away; behold all things are become new* [2 Cor. 5:17].

Further, Paul speaks of the *work of faith*.

> PAUL, and Silvanus, and Timothy, unto the church of the Thessalonians which is in God the Father and in the Lord Jesus Christ: Grace be unto you, and peace, from God our Father, and the Lord Jesus Christ.
> We give thanks to God always for you all, making mention of you in our prayers;
> Remembering without ceasing your work of faith, and labor of love, and patience of hope in our Lord Jesus Christ, in the sight of God and our Father [1 Thess. 1:1–3].
>
> Wherefore also we pray always for you, that our God would count you worthy of this calling, and fulfill all the good pleasure of his goodness, and the work of faith with power [2 Thess. 1:11].
>
> As we have therefore opportunity, let us do good unto all men, especially unto them who are of the household of faith [Gal. 6:10].
>
> For we must all appear before the judgment seat of Christ; that every one may receive the things done in his body, according to that he hath done, whether it be good or bad [2 Cor. 5:10].

The concept of good works is not lacking in the New Testament.

What is the relationship between God's actions and man's good works to bring man into harmony with Him? Another question can be asked: what do good works have to do with justification? Also, what is the thrust of the Reformation with respect to justification?

It concerns the very person of an individual. As noted, God condemns sin. Sin is never permitted in His sight. God sent His only begotten Son and made Him who was without sin into sin for us. *For he hath made him to be sin for us, who knew no sin; that we might be made the righteousness of God in him* [2 Cor. 5:21]. God distinguishes between the sinner and his sin, between the individual's guilty deeds and his sinful state. Therefore, there is an end to sin and its seductive power, but there is not an end to the individual.

Justification is the fact that a person has been accepted by God. How? In Jesus Christ! "The good works are the fruit but not the automatic product of faith," as insightfully expressed by Otto Weber. The good works being discussed result from the act of justification. They are not equal to it.

Justification is a reality that has occurred. The good works are the result of that completed action. Justification happens in the person, and the person does the deeds. Man is justified by the pure grace of God. He does not gain anything with his works. It is God's grace and only God's grace.

We come back again to justification and sanctification. It is not possible to identify the two as one, nor can they be completely separated or polarized. "Justification is not the original cause of sanctification, but rather its constant grounds. Sanctification, in turn, is not just the consequence of justification but rather its living and continual effect in the concrete life of man," as explained by Otto Weber.

The words *just*, *justify*, and *justification* in both the Old Testament and the New Testament are translated by the words "righteous" and "righteousness." These words mean "to declare right," "to become right," and "to make right."

When a person is made right it means he or she is brought into a right relationship with God. Establishing the right relationship between an individual and his or her heavenly Father is by God's grace and only His grace. Consider the following verses:

> *And enter not into judgment with thy servant: for in thy sight shall no man living be justified* [Ps. 143:2].

> *How then can man be justified with God* [Job 25:4]?

Establishing the right relationship between a person and God is by the grace of God, and only by His grace.

The verb translated "justify," *dikaioō*, does not mean "to make just" but belongs to the vocabulary of salvation, or being right with God. What is the necessary condition for justification? It is faith in Christ! It is complete faith, complete trust, and a changed attitude. God's grace works in the individual, and justification is the first step in the salvation process. There is reconciliation to God, which is the beginning of a steady growth in grace and in the knowledge of God.

> *For we are his workmanship* (creation), *created in Christ Jesus unto* (for) *good works, which God hath before ordained* (prepared) *that we should walk in them* [Eph. 2:10].

> *But grow in grace, and in the knowledge of our Lord and Saviour Jesus Christ. To him be glory both now and for ever. Amen* [2 Pet. 3:18].

Peter brings his second letter to a close, with two commands, which are relatively easy to understand. He says, *but grow in grace, and in the knowledge of our Lord and Savior Jesus Christ*. These are not mere suggestions, nor does he place a time limit on obeying them. They are *commands* to be followed through all the days God gives us, because there is no limit to increasing *in grace, and in the knowledge of our Lord and Saviour Jesus Christ*. Walking with Jesus is not for a day, week, or year. It is for a lifetime.

Amen!

3

Called to Walk in His Footsteps

> *I THEREFORE, the prisoner of the Lord, beseech you that ye walk worthy of the vocation* (calling) *wherewith ye are called,* . . . [Eph. 4:1].

The first three chapters of Ephesians are filled with doctrine, with truths allowing us to better understand God's covenant with man, and to reveal the Lord Jesus Christ as God's only Son and our Saviour.

Paul begins the fourth chapter by saying, *I THEREFORE*. What follows is based upon the foundation laid in the first three chapters. He realizes that having a true understanding of doctrine leads to living a holy life.

The Apostle says, *I THEREFORE . . . beseech you that ye walk worthy of the vocation* (calling) *wherewith ye are called*. He uses the word *beseech*. The Greek word is *parakaleō*, which means "to call to one's side." He is saying, "I therefore call you to my side." Think about that!

Paul wants the Ephesians to know the high calling to which they have been called and the importance of it. There are many professing Christians who say they are *in Christ*, but they do not know their calling. They are not maturing as members of Christ's body. They are not increasing in faith and knowledge. They are remaining where they have always been. Their focus is on their own experiences and the ways of the secular world, not upon the Lord Jesus Christ, His commands and teachings. They may say they are going to change their priorities, but they prefer the praise and approval of their contemporaries rather than pleasing God and walking with Jesus. They comply with society's standards, but ignore the fruit of the Spirit. May the power of the Holy Spirit instill in these people the strength of mind, heart, and will to *walk worthy of the vocation* (calling) to which they have been called, that they might know the joy of Christ's blessings, and receive *grace . . . and peace, from God our Father* [Eph. 1:2].

What is the Apostle doing in this first verse? He is saying that the general character of one's life is to endeavor to keep the unity of the spirit in the bond of peace. This approach continues through Ephesians 4:16. After that, he focuses on more direct and practical reasons for applying doctrine to one's daily living.

The Apostle's practice is to lay down general principles and then proceed to the particulars. We go astray when we consider certain particulars by themselves and do not relate them to general principles. The details can be understood only in light of the whole. The whole is greater than any individual parts or several of them together. When specific problems or situations are encountered, they should not be isolated. This approach leads to trouble and misconceptions, which in turn take us down the wrong path. We should be like Paul. Start with the general principle, and then go to the specific items.

Paul urges them to do what? *Walk worthy of the vocation* (calling) *wherewith ye are called*. What did Paul do prior to beseeching them to do this? He described the high calling *in Christ*. He presented the great truths of God and prayed for them. He prayed that God would strengthen them, enable them to comprehend the love of Christ, and have the power that worketh in us. How could they walk worthily without these things happening first?

Yet what happens? People join the church or decide to become active, and they draw upon their own background, experiences, and knowledge instead of learning and acquiring knowledge from Scripture.

What does one do if he or she decides to "*walk worthy*" as a pilot, or engineer, or lawyer, or artist, or whatever vocation he or she may choose to follow? How can you perform without knowing the fundamentals?

Yet many people making a profession of faith or joining a church make this mistake. They try to mend their ways or improve their living without knowing the requirements contained in divine standards. They try to be, before they know what they are to become. You cannot be an accomplished actress, pianist, or golfer without being disciplined in the basic fundamentals.

Certainly, there is great danger to individuals and to the community of believers when doctrine is discarded, ignored, or relegated to a back seat behind experiences. Usually experiences are as unreliable and unacceptable to God as the foundation upon which they are built, which is sand.

What do we prefer to build upon? God's Word and truth, or our own ideas and experiences?

A question: Why does the Apostle use the word *walk* in this verse? Why did he not say "be worthy," or "exercise," or "run," or use some other verb? The word walk in the Greek is *peripateō* and means "to walk around." Think about that for a moment. Paul says, *I . . . beseech you that ye walk worthy of the vocation* (calling), . . . not that you walk around aimlessly after being called.

Paul uses this particular word in the following:

> *For we are his workmanship* (creation), *created in Christ Jesus unto* (for) *good works, which God hath before ordained* (prepared) *that we should walk in them* [Eph. 2:10].

> *This I say therefore, and testify in the Lord, that ye henceforth walk not as other Gentiles walk, in the vanity* (futility) *of their mind, . . .* [Eph. 4:17].

> *See then that ye walk circumspectly* (carefully), *not as fools, but as wise, . . .* [Eph. 5:15].

What does the word *walk* imply? The characteristics of a walk are: a purpose; a goal in mind; progress; advancing steadily; perseverance; steady, sustained motion; and mind, heart, and body in unison. Even if we rest, or pause to admire a view or object, or stop to speak with someone, there is a resolve to continue, and if the road or path becomes arduous and bumpy or the elements such as rain, heat, cold, or snow beset us, we will continue until the goal is reached.

We are going to *walk* through the last three chapters of Ephesians. This *walk* will help us as members of Christ's body through all the days allocated to us, regardless of where the *walk* takes us. God has determined the starting point, the goal, and the pathway, as noted below:

- The beginning of our *walk* is: *According as he hath chosen us in him before the foundation of the world, that we should be holy and without blame before him in love* [Eph. 1:4];
- The goal is: *That he would grant you, according to the riches of his glory, to be strengthened with might by his Spirit in the inner man* [Eph. 3:16]; and

- The pathway is: *And be not drunk with wine, wherein is excess* (dissipation); *but be filled with the Spirit;*

> *Speaking to yourselves in psalms and hymns and spiritual songs, singing and making melody in your heart to the Lord;*
>
> *Giving thanks always for all things unto God and the Father in the name of our Lord Jesus Christ* [Eph. 5:18–20].

How does God want us to *walk*? He wants us to walk according to the Apostle John's direct, enlightening statement that if we keep His word, *in him verily is the love of God perfected.* What a compelling promise! Let these words sink in. Why would we not *keepeth his word*? May we make the proper choice in thought, word, and deed!

> *But whoso keepeth his word, in him verily is the love of God perfected: hereby know we that we are in him.*
> *He that saith he abideth in him ought himself also so to walk, even as he walked* [1 John 2:5–6].

What is God's goal for the members of the community of believers, when they are beseeched to *walk worthy of the vocation* (calling) *wherewith ye are called*? Complete conformity to the image of His Son and for every step they take to bring them closer to Him. This is not an invitation, it is a command!

With whom are we taking the walk? None other than God Himself. This thought is so staggering I scarce can take it in.

What does this walk require? It requires full cooperation, a set purpose, steady progress, perseverance, and step-by-step growth to overcome all opposition.

What type of walk is it? An exceedingly difficult one, but one filled with love and joy; requires meekness and long-suffering; contains hardships and temptations; is beset with worldly currents; offers fellowship with members of the community of believers; and demands a steady, sustained daily consistency.

When embarking upon this walk with God you may find that it is difficult. Jesus had many followers, but only twelve walked with Him the whole way. Would it not be much easier to ignore these things, or to float unconcernedly with the tide of nominal Christianity and drift listlessly with the worldly church, crawl along or sit as a babe and feed only on the milk of elementary doctrines, or soar every now and then to some spiritual heights due to an inspiration or emotion but then relapse when confronted with the realities of life and unsympathetic conditions?

It is easier to assume a task or duty temporarily, than to continuously follow Christ's teachings along life's pathway.

Yes, a daily, consistent walk with Christ is difficult! However, it is beneficial, worthwhile, and rewarding. It is God's way, not man's way.

The dear Apostle devotes much of the last three chapters to telling us about this walk and how worthy it is. The real question is, what are we going to do with the knowledge set before us, and how will we react to the standards established for our conduct?

Will we reject them as being impossible and impractical, or will we receive them as being practical, probable, doable, and livable, and then rejoice in our calling to be members of the community of believers?

Will we pray and ask the Father to send the Spirit through Jesus Christ so that we might walk as He walked?

The next word to consider in our exposition is *worthy*. As mentioned previously, the word means "deserving" or "merited." Some learned authorities tell us this word has two basic ideas.

First, *worthy* conveys the idea of equal weight or balance. They balance perfectly. Therefore, we can say the Apostle is urging the Ephesians to give equal weight or balance to doctrine and to practice.

The second meaning of the word is not to "outweigh" or "tip over" the other. If you pack your head with knowledge, then you are to practice what you have learned.

If your conception of the life *in Christ* is that it only means you are to lead a good life and to be moral, but that doctrine or knowledge is not important, then you become a hindrance to the cause. There must be a true balance.

> *But, beloved, we are persuaded* (confident of) *better things of* (concerning) *you, and things that accompany salvation, though we thus speak.*
> *For God is not unrighteous to forget your work and labor of love, which ye have showed toward his name, in that ye have ministered to the saints, and do minister.*
> *And we desire that every one of you do show the same diligence to the full assurance of hope unto the end:*
> *That ye be not slothful* (sluggish), *but followers* (imitators) *of them who through faith and patience inherit the promises* [Heb. 6:9–12].

The author of this great letter commends the followers for their diligence on the practical side, then he urges them to show the same diligence in grasping the doctrines of the faith and that *You do show the same diligence to the full assurance of hope unto the end* [Heb. 6:11].

These verses show we are to love others and to perform works for others due to the gifts God has given to us and knowing that He fulfills His promises. Therefore, we are to minister unto the saints. On the other side of the coin, our faith is to correspond to our love and works. Yes, you should fulfill your obligations to men, but it is more important to apply yourself "with no less zeal to progress in your faith, so as to show God its full and firm certainty," according to John Calvin as he encourages us to commit to maturing in our faith.

The author in these verses shows that there are two distinct parts to our life *in Christ*. You cannot separate the two sides of the same coin. If you do, one side or the other is going to be torn and mutilated, and you are robbing God of His pre-eminent rights.

Why does the author of the letter to the Hebrews say *the full assurance of hope unto the end*? First, because some professing faith in Christ were being distracted by opinions, superstitions, doubts, and false teachings. The author stresses that the truth of God is unwavering. Since it is the faith of those relying upon Him who are members of the community of believers, they should be true, sure, firm, and above all have no doubts regarding God, His promises, and their faith in Him.

Hope as it is used here is in the sense of faith. True faith always goes hand in hand with hope. The author of Hebrews calls them to be followers and imitators . . . *of them who through faith and patience inherit the promises* [Heb. 6:12].

Their fathers were partakers in the promises only by the grace of God and "by the unconquered firmness of their faith," as Calvin explicitly states what is required of each professing Christian. When we are exposed to doctrine and see how it is fulfilled in Paul, Peter, Abraham, and others, then we begin to assimilate it, understand it, and apply it.

Second, another idea contained in the word *worthy* is *becoming*.

> *Only let your conversation* (conduct be worthy of) *be as it becometh the gospel of Christ: that whether I come and see you, or else be absent, I may hear of your affairs, that ye stand fast in one spirit, with one mind striving together for the faith of the gospel* [Phil. 1:27].

Note the first portion of this verse. The word *becometh* in the Greek is *axios*. Also, in Ephesians 4:1 the word *worthy* in the Greek is *axios*. The same word. The proper interpretation for the word *conversation* is "tenor of life." Therefore, Philippians 1:27 should read "only let the tenor of your life be as it becometh, or is worthy of, the Gospel of Christ." The idea expressed in Ephesians 4:1 and Philippians 1:27 is the same.

There is not to be a clash between doctrine and practice. Paul in writing to Titus says doctrine has little authority unless its power and majesty shine in the life of a follower. Paul urges Titus to follow the doctrines that have been given to him in order that his way of life may reflect his teaching. Paul wants his good works to reflect the doctrines. He tells Timothy,

> *In all things showing thyself a pattern of good works: in doctrine showing uncorruptness* (integrity), *gravity* (reverence), *sincerity* (incorruptibility),
> *Sound speech, that cannot be condemned* [Titus 2:7–8].

He makes it clear to Titus that his honorable behavior in daily living *adorns the doctrine of God*, which is a reflection of His glory. He amplifies upon this writing, *Not purloining* (pilfering), *but showing all good fidelity; that they may adorn the doctrine of God our Saviour in all things* [Titus 2:10]. This applies to you and to me. We are to live the type of life that will *adorn the doctrine of God*.

As we continue through Ephesians 4:1, Paul tells us that the doctrine is to be our vocation, saying, *I therefore, . . . beseech you that ye walk worthy of the vocation* (calling) *wherewith ye are called*. What does the word *vocation* mean, and what does the doctrine convey? The word *vocation* appears only this one time in Scripture. The Greek word is *klēsis* and it is from the same root as the Greek word for church, *ecclesia*. *Klēsis* means "a calling," whereas *ecclesia* means "the called-out ones."

The doctrine it conveys is that we are to live a certain type of life because we have been "called." A member of the community of believers must never be thought of as someone who has decided to take up a certain life. The life *in Christ* is never to be thought of as something we decide to take up. It is the exact opposite. We have been called. Actually, this verse should read, "that ye walk worthy of the calling wherewith ye are called."

Therefore, we should always remember that we have been called. It is not our own doing. Paul tells us that God has blessed us and chosen us. He expands upon this, saying, *According as he hath chosen us in him before the foundation of the world, that we should be holy and without blame before him in love* [Eph. 1:4].

The primary reason we are to live a holy and sanctified life is that we are the *called ones*. Yes, we can all agree, whether we are members of the community of believers or not, that it is the right thing to do, that we are not to sin, and it is right to live the *Christian life*. These are admirable thoughts.

However, the reason for living a holy life is that we have been "called." We have been chosen by God the Father through our Lord Jesus Christ to *be holy and without blame before him in love*. We are to respond positively by being obedient to His call and His commands. It is an awesome responsibility!

What does Scripture reveal concerning a "call" or "being called"? There are two types. One is a general call made to everyone, as in *but now* (God) *commandeth all men every where to repent* [Acts 17:30], and the other is the effective call to repent and to believe the gospel.

Those who hear or are aware of the general call can be divided unto two groups: those remaining unbelievers, and those effectively responding to the call. The latter are the ones that become members of the community of believers.

> *For the wrath of God is revealed from heaven against all ungodliness and unrighteousness of men, who hold* (suppress) *the truth in unrighteousness;*
> *Because that which may be known of God is manifest* (evident) *in* (among) *them; for God hath showed it unto them.*
> *For the invisible things of him from the creation of the world are clearly seen, being understood by the things that are made, even his eternal power and Godhead* (Divine Nature); *so that they are without excuse:*
> *Because that, when they knew God, they glorified him not as God, neither were thankful; but became vain* (futile) *in their imaginations* (thoughts), *and their foolish heart was darkened.*
> *Professing themselves to be wise, they became fools,*
> *And changed the glory of the uncorruptible God into an image made like to corruptible* (perishable) *man, and to birds, and fourfooted beasts, and creeping things.*

> *Wherefore God also gave them up to uncleanness through the lusts of their own hearts, to dishonor their own bodies between themselves:*
> *Who changed* (exchanged) *the truth of God into a lie* (for a lie), *and worshipped and served the creature more* (rather) *than the Creator, who is blessed for ever. Amen* [Rom. 1:18-25].

To some, the preaching of the Cross is foolishness, it is a stumbling block. To others, those receiving an effective call, it is the power and wisdom of God. There is a fundamental distinction between the two groups.

You may ask the question, when does the effective call come?

> *Moreover whom he did predestinate, them he also called: and whom he called, them he also justified: and whom he justified, them he also glorified* [Rom. 8:30].

Whom He did predestinate, He called; whom He called, He justified; and whom He justified, He glorified.

Salvation is initiated by and the result of the Spirit of God acting within a person, enabling one to believe, introducing a new way of life, and strengthening one to live the new life in Christ Jesus.

We are called to believe. Jesus says, *No man can come to me, except the Father which hath sent me draw him* [John 6:44]. The "call" draws the person. The power is in the "call."

Consider the relationship between Lydia and Paul. Lydia's heart was opened by the Lord. After her heart was opened the Word became effective. *AND you hath he quickened* (made alive), *who were dead in trespasses and sins* [Eph. 2:1]. A dead person cannot quicken himself. However, God can and He does so by an effective "call." We see this in Jesus calling Lazarus from the tomb. We see this in Abraham and Sarah.

Look at what Peter says,

> *Being born again, not of corruptible* (perishable) *seed, but of incorruptible* (imperishable), *by the word of God, which liveth and abideth for ever* [1 Pet. 1:23].

> *But ye are a chosen generation, a royal priesthood, a holy nation, a peculiar* (his own special) *people; that ye should show* (proclaim) *forth the praises of him who hath called you out of darkness into his marvelous light* [1 Pet. 2:9].

Paul urges us to *walk worthy of the vocation* (calling) *wherewith ye are called* [Eph. 4:1]. How are we to do this? This question is directed to each of us. It is not to be glossed over and placed in that never, never land of "Let go, let God." It is to be digested, pondered, and applied with forethought and diligence. It is an individual responsibility, one that is not to be shirked. Therefore, we are to conduct ourselves by acquiring knowledge, applying doctrine, and realizing we have been "called" by God Himself, not the Church, nor the minister, nor family, nor friend, but by God Almighty; reminding ourselves of these things in order to increase in faith and understanding; and acknowledging we have been called to this great, high calling, and our lives are to be in accord with it.

These are monumental truths for professing Christians and for walking with Jesus. Therefore, to help us on our way, we should always remember:

> *Blessed be the God and Father of our Lord Jesus Christ, who hath blessed us with all spiritual blessings in heavenly places in Christ:*
> *According as he hath chosen us in him before the foundation of the world, that we should be holy and without blame before him in love:*
> *Having predestinated us unto the adoption of children* (as sons) *by Jesus Christ to himself, according to the good pleasure of his will,* ... [Eph. 1:3–5].

This is what matters: He *who hath blessed us*, not the problems and difficulties we encounter. The blessings are in Christ Jesus.

God called us not to keep us from something or that we may be moral, law-abiding, friendly, and nice. We are adopted as children by Jesus Christ Himself. He called us to *be holy and without blame before Him*. That is what we are to become!

These truths are very powerful and should have an impact upon us, if they have not already. Remember, we have been adopted, we are members of the family, we are heirs, joint heirs with Christ. Unfortunately, these are things we forget in the hustle and bustle of daily living. Therefore, we need to constantly remind ourselves of them.

We are to remember that Christ dwells in our hearts by faith, and that there is to be the fullness of God in us. This is the way to sanctification, to holiness, and to realizing these things are true.

How does this calling take place? What makes it possible? It is the gift of God, not of works. We are His workmanship, no longer aliens and strangers having no hope. *Ye who sometimes were far off, are made nigh by the blood of Christ* [Eph. 2:13].

When we are tempted or downcast or have a case of the "woebegones," we are to remember how the call came and the price paid for it. We are to remember the power given to us.

> *And what is the exceeding greatness of his power to us-ward who believe, according to the working of his mighty power, . . .* [Eph. 1:19].

> *That he would grant you, according to the riches of his glory, to be strengthened with might by his Spirit in the inner man* [Eph. 3:16].

> *Now unto him that is able to do exceeding abundantly above all that we ask or think, according to the power that worketh in us, . . .* [Eph. 3:20].

We are to *walk worthy of the calling wherewith ye have been called.* We have no right to live as we please or choose.

> *What? Know ye not that your body is the temple of the Holy Ghost which is in you, which ye have of God, and ye are not your own?*
>
> *For ye are bought with a price: therefore glorify God in your body, and in your spirit, which are God's* [1 Cor. 6:19–20].

Paul does three things in these two verses. First, he asks a question regarding the Holy Ghost, God the Father, and each of us.

Second, he goes to the heart of the matter and tells us that we have been *bought with a price* by Christ being crucified. And third, he commands us to glorify God in our bodies, and in our spirits. Why? Because they are God's, and He gave them to us.

We are prisoners of the Lord Jesus Christ, and thank God we are. We have been called to His side, and we are to act *worthy of the vocation* (calling) *wherewith ye are called.*

Amen!

4

Unity

> *With all lowliness and meekness* (gentleness), *with long-suffering, forbearing* (bearing with) *one another in love;*
> *Endeavoring to keep the unity of the Spirit in the bond of peace*
> [Eph. 4:2–3].

We are to realize *with all lowliness and meekness* (gentleness) that we have been *called,* and therefore we are to walk worthy of that calling. The Apostle ends this first sentence saying, *Endeavoring to keep the unity of the Spirit in the bond of peace.*

Why does he stress the *unity of the Spirit*? A strong trait of Christ's calling is preserving the *unity of the Spirit*. We should remember this as we strive to *walk worthy* of our calling. This is important. Paul devotes much time in verses two through sixteen to the question of unity.

Why is unity important? The harmonious spiritual functioning of all members of Christ's body depends upon perfect coordination. When we are physically ill, our coordination suffers. When there are spiritual maladjustments among the community of believers or among the members of a particular congregation, then sin takes hold, and attention is focused upon secondary matters. When this happens our Lord is dishonored, His work suffers, and we are the losers. Therefore, we are to proceed in this calling *With all lowliness and meekness* (gentleness), *with long-suffering, forbearing* (bearing with) *one another in love;* . . . *endeavoring to keep the unity of the Spirit in the bond of peace.*

First, we should examine the character of unity. The Apostle is not appealing for a general spirit of friendship or camaraderie nor for a common objective, nor is he urging support against a common enemy.

Much of the talk today about unity is vague or nebulous, or in terms describing the world as being divided. Others say that all those believing in God should join together and act together. They also say it is not important what one believes, but it is important to have a spirit of fellowship and friendship, and to work together against a common enemy.

However, what the Apostle speaks about is a unity resulting directly from the doctrines and prayers contained in the first three chapters. You cannot have true unity *in Christ* unless it is based upon the doctrines presented and the love described in those chapters.

People say it does not matter what you believe or what knowledge you acquire, as long as you call yourself a Christian or believe in God in any sense whatsoever.

What should be our response? In response, Martyn Lloyd-Jones asks, "My dear sir or madam, what about the first three chapters of Ephesians?" There is no real unity unless the foundation is built upon the doctrine and love presented in those chapters.

Whatever unity Paul describes, it is to be based upon doctrine, truth, Christ's love, and the fullness of God. That is to be the foundation.

The unity to which we are called is defined as follows:

- it is not a unity of denominations or a federation of church bodies;
- we are united to Christ through the baptism of the Spirit;
- membership in Christ's body is maintained by the indwelling Spirit, which is God's doing, not ours;
- we have a responsibility regarding the outreaching of God's eternal purpose;
- we have a responsibility regarding the manifestation of Christ's glory and person;
- these responsibilities require working effectually with others; and
- God calls us to keep the unity, the unity in the Spirit.

"God is not asking us to make unity, but He is asking us to keep the unity that already exists," as properly expressed by Ruth Paxson.

Paul is referring to and identifying the Holy Spirit. He is not describing a human spirit or community spirit or social spirit. He is identifying the Holy Spirit. This unity, of which Paul speaks, is created and indwelt by the Holy Spirit. It is a spiritual fellowship *in Christ* that shares His life, purpose, and power.

Every member of the *community of believers* should be determined to keep this unity. Each of us should do our utmost to be effective custodians of our inheritance and the blessings received at Pentecost. Such unity is dependent upon specifically stated doctrines that are neither intangible nor uncertain. "The basis (of this unity) is in truth, and the bond is in love," as Ruth Paxson clearly expresses the two most important characteristics for living as Christ would have us live. This is important, accurate, and challenging. It is rooted in God's truth, becomes fruitful in God's love, and challenges us to acquire knowledge, exhibit His love, and obey His commands. It is produced and created by the Holy Spirit. We cannot do it. However, we are not to break it, we are to maintain it.

It is important to know and agree upon: the Doctrine of the Holy Spirit; regeneration; and being a new creature *in Christ*. It is believing in the revelation of the Holy Spirit's work, as contained in Scripture.

This is entirely different from the idea that Christianity means doing good works, or being moral, ethical, "religious," or taking an interest in a local church or denomination, or participating in certain activities.

There is one thing to recognize and accept about the Lord Jesus Christ,

> *For he* (himself) *is our peace, who hath made both one, and hath broken down the middle wall of partition* (division) *between us* [Eph. 2:14].

This unity is experienced when the Holy Spirit works in both parties. It is basic and fundamental. It is unseen, and it is internal.

However, it expresses itself visibly and externally. Members of the community of believers belong to churches together. They study together, and they work together. It is important for the Spirit to work within each one, and to allow each one to give a positive expression to the fruit of the Spirit.

> *But the fruit of the Spirit is love, joy, peace, long-suffering, gentleness* (kindness), *goodness, faith* (faithfulness),
> *Meekness* (gentleness), *temperance* (self-control): *against such there is no law.*
> *And they that are Christ's have crucified the flesh with the affections* (passions) *and lusts.*

> *If we live in the Spirit, let us also walk in the Spirit*
> *Let us not be desirous* (conceited) *of vain glory, provoking one another, envying one another* [Gal. 5:22–26].

Today and for the past several decades there has been a consistent appeal for ecumenicity. The appeal has been for previously divided people or groups to act together, to work together, to pray together, and pretty soon they will feel like they have unity.

There is some truth to that, where the Holy Spirit is working and has been working in both parties and where the middle wall or partition has been broken down. But it is not true in every situation. Therefore, an amplification of the Apostle's teaching is required.

When thinking about creation, or reproduction, you soon recognize that the internal comes first, and then the external. What does this mean? Consider, if you will, "two very small cells contain the life out of which a complete body will develop. A body does not consist of a collection of parts or items loosely or haphazardly joined together. They are *fitly framed together*. Each part of the body develops and grows out of the central life," to paraphrase Martyn Lloyd-Jones.

The same principle is true of unity in the Spirit. First, the internal, then the external. The unity of the Spirit cannot be seen, or touched or placed on display. However, when it is present, we experience it, both in ourselves and in others with whom we may have fellowship.

How do we *keep the unity of the Spirit in the bond of peace*? The principles for so doing have a beautiful, simple ring to them, but practicing them day in and day out requires contemplation and the realization that we (me and you) must exercise the necessary effort by:

- being diligent;
- acquiring humility, which is one of the primary virtues resulting from being poor in spirit;
- exhibiting meekness, which is an inner mildness and gentleness, yet appropriately exhibiting true strength (Moses was meek, yet he had immense strength);
- becoming long-suffering, which is suffering long, and not giving way to passion or emotions;

- developing forbearance, forbearing which is *to hold yourself up against* a wrong attitude, action, or temptation and to endure, suffer, and bear up against life's difficulties;
- exercising self-control;
- learning to be patient; and
- doing these things in love.

That is the clincher, or should I say "clunker." We are not born with these fruits of the Spirit, but by God's grace and power may they become an integral part of your heart, mind, and personality as well as mine.

Learning to do in love is difficult, especially when you have been offended or do not like someone, but by the strength of the Holy Spirit we are to develop and exhibit it under negative as well as positive conditions.

Paul, under the influence of the Holy Spirit, says we are to endeavor with all lowliness, meekness, long-suffering, and forbearing to keep the unity of the Spirit in the bond of peace, but then he has the audacity or, if you will, the cool, calm, composure to say we are to do all this to others *in love*.

It is difficult to do any of the first five things individually, but when Paul adds *in love* he complicates matters. Do you see why it is important to read each phrase, each verse? Do you see why it is important to understand what the Apostle says in detail?

Previously, we spent considerable time defining and describing what the Apostle meant by lowliness, meekness, long-suffering, forbearing and endeavoring.

Guess what happened to me? During the subsequent period, the Lord tested me. He tested me, tested me, and tested me. He gave me a dose, and what I thought was an overdose, of trials and tests that could only be handled by endeavoring with lowliness, meekness, long-suffering, and forbearing. That is God's way.

Therefore, be prepared. Remember, as we proceed to examine God's Word you and I are going to be tested! Thank God that He loves us and will do that.

The Apostle says if we manifest those characteristics then we are preserving the unity. Think what we are doing when we exhibit these traits. We are acting as peacemakers. We are being peaceable. Think of the Beatitudes:

- *Blessed are the poor in Spirit:*
- *Blessed are they that mourn:*
- *Blessed are the meek:*
- *Blessed are they which do hunger and thirst after righteousness:*
- *Blessed are the merciful:*
- *Blessed are the pure in heart:* and
- *Blessed are the peacemakers*

[Selections from Matt. 5:3–9].

These are the characteristics of the person *in Christ* and of the members of the community of believers. This is the calling to which we have been called.

The end of all doctrine is to preserve this *unity of the Spirit in the bond of peace*. The end of all conduct is exactly the same: faith, application, doctrine, and practice. The Apostle is saying: do not quench the Spirit, and do not grieve the Spirit. Allow the Spirit to produce His own glorious fruit in you.

> *But the fruit of the Spirit is love, joy, peace, long-suffering, gentle-*ness (kindness), *goodness, faith* (faithfulness),
> *Meekness, temperance* (self-control): *against such there is no law* [Gal. 5:22–23].

Now that the Apostle, under the influence of the Holy Spirit, has charged us with a sacred responsibility, he proceeds to tell us how to do it. He amplifies upon this through a sevenfold presentation saying,

> *. . . one body, and one Spirit, . . . one hope;*
> *One Lord, one faith, one baptism,*
> *One God and Father of all, who is above all, and through all, and in you all* [Eph. 4:4–6].

In addition to walking in unity, we will examine the other facets of this walk: holiness, love, light, wisdom, praise, and harmony.

May this walk produce abundant fruit in each and every one.
Amen!

5

One Body, and One Spirit

There is one body, and one Spirit, even as ye are called in one hope of your calling;
  One Lord, one faith, one baptism,
  One God and Father of all, who is above all, and through all, and in you all [Eph. 4:4–6].

The first three verses of the fourth chapter are a continuation of what the Apostle has been presenting in the first half of this magnificent letter. He beseeched the members of the community *to do certain things and to keep the unity of the Spirit*. These verses set the foundation for the practical truths contained in verses 4–16 of this chapter, beginning with

  . . . *one body, and one Spirit, even as ye are called in one hope of your calling;*
  One Lord, one faith, one baptism,
  One God and Father of all, who is above all, and through all, and in you all.

Paul emphasizes the word *one*. He emphasizes unity. He repeats it and establishes the principle of essential unity in the community of believers. The word *one* occurs seven times in three verses. This suggests the number of the Divinity and of perfection. It is not often stressed, but it should be.

It reminds us of Genesis, the first and second chapters. Possibly Paul (and this is speculation) wanted us to see that the unity of the community of believers is a manifestation of the Godhead's perfection.

There are three groupings in these verses and they are arranged around the Holy Trinity: the first three belong to the Holy Spirit, the second three belong to the Lord Jesus Christ, and the last one is God the Father Himself.

When digesting this, we should grasp the doctrine of unity and realize its importance in our daily lives. It should allow us to comprehend and grasp the blessed Holy Trinity, the three in One, the One in three. The church is to be a reflection of the blessed Holy Trinity.

"Our Lord never asked for a man-made union of organized churches into a grand federation, but He prayed for a Spirit-made, Christ-centered, God controlled unity in the living organism, The Body of Christ," according to Ruth Paxson.

Why does the Apostle start with the Holy Spirit, proceed to the Lord Jesus Christ, and then to the Father?

> First, he starts with the Holy Spirit to show that the community of believers is in fellowship with the Spirit. He starts with us where we are and as we are. Then he moves to higher ground, to the head, who is Christ. He moves us from being indwelt by the Spirit, to the one and only Mediator, and then to God the Father.
>
> Second, he shows that we exist and have our being due to the Holy Spirit. However, the Holy Spirit would not have come if it had not been for the Son and what He did. And certainly, the Son would not have come if it had not been for the Father.
>
> Third, the Spirit leads us to the Son, and the Son leads us to the Father.

> *Likewise the Spirit also helpeth our infirmities (weaknesses): for we know not what we should pray for as we ought: but the Spirit itself maketh intercession for us with groanings which cannot be uttered.*
>
> *And he that searcheth the hearts knoweth what is the mind of the Spirit, because he maketh intercession for the saints according to the will of God* [Rom. 8:26–27].

"Paul has appropriately connected prayers with the anxious desires of the godly, because God does not afflict them with troubles in order that they may inwardly feed on hidden grief, but that they may unburden themselves by prayer and thus exercise their faith.

"*But the Spirit Himself maketh intercession for us.* Although it may not yet appear in fact that our prayers have been heard by God, Paul concludes that the presence of heavenly grace already shines forth in the very zeal for prayer, because no one of his own accord conceives devout and godly prayers . . . . The Spirit, therefore, must prescribe the manner of our praying. Paul calls the groans into which we break forth by the impulse of the Spirit unutterable, because they far exceed the capacity of our intellect. [Further] he affects our hearts in such a way that these prayers penetrate into heaven itself by their fervency. Paul has spoken in this way for the purpose of attributing the whole of prayer more significantly to the grace of the Spirit.

"The fact that we are heard by God while we pray through His Spirit is a notable reason for confirming our confidence, for He Himself is intimately acquainted with our prayers, as being the thoughts of His own Spirit . . . It follows from this that that which is agreeable to His will, by which all things are ruled, cannot be inefficacious. Let us also learn from this that the first part of prayer is consent to the will of the Lord, who is by no means bound to follow our desires. We must, therefore, pray to God to regulate our prayers according to His will, if we would have them accepted by Him," as expounded upon by John Calvin.

The Apostle demonstrates that there should not be any argument about *the unity of the Spirit in the bond of peace*. Why? Because the unity is already there in one body.

The Apostle is not appealing to us to form this unity. He tells us that the unity is already there, and that we are to keep it. He urges us not to break it in any way. Paul reminds us in the fourth verse that we are members of the community. He does this by reminding the Ephesians that *there is one body*.

A careful examination of Paul's letters reveals he uses the term *body* in referring to Christ's church in the following ways:

> *And hath put all things under his feet, and gave him to be the head over all things to the church,*
> *Which is his body, the fullness of him that filleth all in all* [Eph. 1:22–23].

> *And that he might reconcile both unto God in one body by the cross, having slain* (put to death) *the enmity thereby* [Eph. 2:16].

> *There is one body, and one Spirit, even as ye are called in one hope of your calling* [Eph. 4:4].

> *For the perfecting* (equipping) *of the saints, for the work of the ministry, for the edifying of the body of Christ* [Eph. 4:12].

> *For we are members of his body, of his flesh, and of his bones* [Eph. 5:30].
>
> *And he is the head of the body, the church: who is the beginning, the first-born from the dead; that in all things he might have the pre-eminence* [Col. 1:18].

What does the Apostle mean by referring to the church or community as *one body*? Note that he does not say "one church." If Paul had used that term then undoubtedly one of the large churches within Christendom would have declared that that distinction applied to them. Certainly, even a small sect or denomination could make such a claim.

Ephesians teaches that, yes, there is one body, eternal in calling, divine in creation, and supernatural in its constitution. The members of this body have been called out of every circumstance, country, people, and culture. They differ in many, many ways: language, color, training, education, ability, temperament, likes, dislikes, prejudices, and many other categories. Yet through the blood of the Saviour and the baptism of the Spirit, they are united *in Christ* as living members of His body.

The members of the community of believers exist in the body of Christ. He does not exist without His community and the community does not exist without Him. The community, you and me, exists in the reality of the present Christ. He is not one who was "once upon a time," nor is He one that will be sometime in the future. He is always in the present.

This concept of the body of Christ appears in Paul's letters. The term *body* is a real and active form and is often used with either the phrase *in Christ* or *with Christ*:

> *For as the body is one, and hath many members, and all the members of that one body, being many, are one body: so also is Christ* [1 Cor. 12:12].
>
> *For we being many are one bread, and one body: for we are all partakers of that one bread* [1 Cor. 10:17].
>
> FOR MOSES DESCRIBETH (WRITES ABOUT) THE RIGHTEOUSNESS WHICH IS OF THE LAW, THAT THE MAN WHICH DOETH THOSE THINGS SHALL LIVE BY THEM [Rom. 10:5].

There is neither Jew nor Greek, there is neither bond (slave) *nor free, there is neither male nor female: for ye are all one in Christ Jesus* [Gal. 3:28].

And let the peace of God rule in your hearts, to the which also ye are called in one body; and be ye thankful [Col. 3:15].

Second, . . . *that he might reconcile both unto God in one body by the cross, having slain* (put to death) *the enmity thereby* [Eph. 2:16].

"This unity is not the result of people or groups deciding to come together, but is based upon losing their earlier existence. It occurs when you come under the influence of the One who was crucified."

Ye also are become dead to the law by the body of Christ [Rom. 7:4].

"Being incorporated into the body of Christ means participating in His death and participating in His life."

Likewise reckon (consider) *ye also yourselves to be dead indeed unto sin, but alive unto God through* (in) *Jesus Christ our Lord.*
Let not sin therefore reign in your mortal body, that ye should obey it in the lusts thereof.
Neither yield (present) *ye your members as instruments of unrighteousness unto sin: but yield* (present) *yourselves unto God, as those that are alive from the dead, and your members as instruments* (weapons) *of righteousness unto God.*
For sin shall not have dominion over you: for ye are not under the law, but under grace.
What then? shall we sin, because we are not under the law, but under grace? God forbid (certainly not).
Know ye not, that to whom ye yield (present*) yourselves servants to obey, his servants* (slaves) *ye are to whom ye obey; whether of sin unto death, or of obedience unto righteousness?*
But God be thanked, that (though) *ye were the servants* (slaves) *of sin, but ye have obeyed from the heart that form of doctrine which was delivered you* (to which you were entrusted).
Being then made free from sin, ye became the servants of righteousness [Rom. 6:11–18].

For as many of you as have been baptized into Christ have put on Christ [Gal. 3:27].

"Third, the body of Christ, given up to death, and the body of the community are conceived of together, yet it is difficult to explain." Consider,

In the body of his flesh through death, to present you holy and unblamable and unreprovable in his sight [Col. 1:22].

Paul writes to the Ephesians, stating,

And that he might reconcile both unto God in one body by the cross, having slain (put to death) *the enmity thereby* [Eph. 2:16].

And to the Corinthians he says,

I speak as to wise men; judge ye what I say.
The cup of blessing which we bless, is it not the communion (fellowship) *of the blood of Christ? The bread which we break, is it not the communion (fellowship) of the body of Christ?*
For we being many are one bread, and one body: for we are all partakers of that one bread [1 Cor. 10:15–17].

Paul begins this portion of Corinthians by giving them encouragement. He appeals to their egos. He tells them they are wise, that he is not addressing them as babes or as ones to whom the gospel has not been revealed.

"You are well aware of the power of the Holy Supper, for in it we are in-grafted into the Body of the Lord," as John Calvin appropriately informs us regarding this important truth.

In these verses, Paul begins with the second of the two sacramental elements. He calls it *the cup of blessing*. It means setting it apart for one purpose, that it might be a sign for all believers that Christ's blood was shed for them.

The cup of blessing is communion through the blood of Christ. It means that the believers are bound together by the blood of Christ. For what reason? So that they might become one body. This unity is properly called communion. Paul says, *For we being many are one bread, and one body: for we are all partakers of that one body* [1 Cor. 10:17].

Why is it important to be united with Christ? Because it is necessary to be incorporated into Him first if we are to be united to each other. Paul is discussing not a mere human relationship, but a union in the Spirit between Christ and the believers.

It is by *the cup of blessing*, the blood of Christ, that we are grafted into His body. It is by this means that He lives in us and we live in Him.

The broken bread is participation in the body of Christ. This participation, this fellowship, means implicitly a new existence. This is the same as being incorporated into the community of believers.

Reformed theology, following the lead of Calvin, understands that faith is "insertion in Christ." Believing in Jesus Christ does not just mean that some mystical union will take place, but in essence it means membership in His body.

Paul explains this to the Corinthians, saying,

> Always bearing about in the body the dying of the Lord Jesus, that the life also of Jesus might be made manifest in our body [2 Cor. 4:10].

He amplifies upon it, saying to the Philippians and the Romans,

> That I may know him, and the power of his resurrection, and the fellowship of his sufferings, being made conformable unto his death [Phil. 3:10]?

> And if children, then heirs; heirs of God, and joint-heirs with Christ; if so be that we suffer with him, that we may be also glorified together [Rom. 8:17].

These portions of Scripture refer to not only something spiritual or in the Spirit, but to something physical, to human existence in its most concrete form. We are joint heirs with Christ. If we live as He would have us to live, He will guide us and guard us through the Holy Spirit, and we will be glorified with Him.

Christ being the head of the body is expanded upon in Ephesians and Colossians. Also, the community being under the Head, Jesus Christ Himself. "The Community is related to its Lord and Head in a one-sidedly determined unity: it is not its own lord or its own head. Because Jesus Christ is its Lord and Head, it lives not its own life, but His life," according to Otto Weber as he clarifies the role of the community of believers with respect to the Lord Jesus.

Bear in mind the one pertinent fact that we are members of Christ's body. It is possible for a person to be a member of the visible church, but not to be a member of the unseen church, the community of believers.

There are certain things to understand regarding the invisible church, the body of Christ. First is the organic character of the unity that is the community. The community, or the church as we call it, is a new creation.

God brought the community into being. He did not bring some Jews and Gentiles together and have them agree on an agenda and a white paper. No, that is not His way. He created it. He brought into being a new creation. He did not assemble different groups and ask them to agree.

Paul identifies the two groups in order to emphasize that the difference in background or condition is not an obstacle to unity in the Spirit or as members of the community.

The middle wall of partition is broken down and God creates *of twain one new man*. This can be seen in Paul's analogy to the Corinthians regarding Christ's body, its different parts and its unity, when he says,

> For as the body is one, and hath many members, and all the members of that one body, being many, are one body: so also is Christ.
>
> *For by one Spirit are we all baptized into one body, whether we be Jews or Gentiles (Greeks), whether we be bond (slaves) or free; and have been all made to drink into one Spirit* [1 Cor. 12:12–13].
>
> *And whether (if) one member suffer, all the members suffer with it; or one member be honored, all the members rejoice with it.*
> Now ye are the body of Christ, and members in particular (individually) [1 Cor. 12: 26–27].

Of what does the body consist? Two hands, arms, and feet, ten fingers and toes, two eyes and ears. However, the body is not a collection of parts. It starts as a single cell, which develops and grows, and as it does it forms the different parts.

It does not occur the other way around. The true church is a new creation. Those who belong to her are born of the Spirit and of Christ. This is something we are to understand. It enables us to grasp the unity. However, it is difficult when we are accustomed to thinking of the church as a building with its membership rolls.

The second point the Apostle emphasizes is diversity in unity. What we see in the community is unity, not uniformity. Recall Paul writing to the Corinthians, saying, *That some say, I am of Paul, I of Apollos, I of Cephus, and I of Christ* [1 Cor. 1:12].

Paul was addressing the Corinthians' contentiousness, wrangling, and arguing. This was Paul's way of telling them that they had forgotten that the church is the body of Christ.

He ridicules them and then teaches the principle that in the church or community, there is diversity in unity, just as there is in the human body. Remember, there is unity, not uniformity.

Third, there is interdependence. Not one part has any real meaning or existence on its own. What makes the body a body is that all the various parts are in reality one. They have an essential unity and are interdependent upon one another. Certainly there is no independence in the body. Each part needs the other to function as a body. Each one benefits the other.

Fourth, every single member is important. This is true of the body. It is true of the members of the community. Each is important; each has a function to perform. Each member is essential to the harmonious working of both the physical body and the body of Christ. Whether that person sits in the pew, works in the visible church, or preaches from the pulpit.

In the community, both the people and the actions matter. Anything that cuts across the idea of interdependence or the importance of all the parts of the body is not only contrary to New Testament doctrine, but introduces divisions, schisms and disharmony.

Fifth, all parts of the body work in unison and toward the same objective, even though each part has its own function.

The church, or the community, is the body of Christ. We are members of that body. It is through the church, or the called out, that God reveals His will. Paul says, *To the intent that now unto the principalities and powers in heavenly places might be known by the church the manifold* (many-sided) *wisdom of God* [Eph. 3:10]. It is through the community, each and everyone of us, that God reveals Himself.

As we close this portion, remember one thing. If one member suffers, then all suffer. If there is pain in your little finger, it goes throughout the entire body and affects it.

If we truly understand New Testament teaching, we know who is the active head of the church. Any idea other than serving Him is ludicrous. In that category are such things as self-importance, self-serving rivalry, and competition. The way to avoid these things is to understand doctrine and Christ's teachings. Remember, we are members of the body of Christ. There is only one body. He is the Head, and we are the members. We are *in Christ*, and we belong to Him.

Amen!

6

The Person of the Holy Spirit

> *There is one body, and one Spirit, even as ye are called in one hope of your calling* [Eph. 4:4].

Paul begins by saying *one body*. Then he focuses attention on *one Spirit*. If the church is the body of Christ and if it is like a body,

"Where has it come from?
Why was it formed?
What constitutes its life?
What makes it a vital, living organism?
What enables it to function?"

The Apostle answers these questions by saying, "The Holy Spirit. The church, or the body of Christ, is the result of the Holy Spirit's activity. The Holy Spirit operates in the church and maintains its life and well-being," according to Martyn Lloyd-Jones.

The Apostle wants to show that the unity of the community of believers is possible because the Holy Spirit is not only at the center of it but permeates its very life and being. "The crux of what the Apostle says in this particular phrase is that there is *one Spirit*. There is only one Holy Spirit, and He is indivisible," as stated by Martyn Lloyd-Jones.

However, there are many evil spirits. We are reminded of this when Paul says,

> *For we wrestle not against flesh and blood, but against principalities, against powers, against the rulers of the darkness of this world* (age), *against spiritual* (hosts of) *wickedness in high places* [Eph. 6:12].

Note a significant point. He is called the Holy Spirit, which differentiates Him from all other spirits.

Consider two situations in the Gospels.

> *But when he saw Jesus afar off, he ran and worshipped him.*
> *And cried with a loud voice, and said, What have I to do with thee, Jesus, thou Son of the most high God? I adjure* (implore) *thee by God, that thou torment me not.*
> *For he said unto him, Come out of the man, thou unclean spirit.*
> *And he asked him, What is thy name? And he answered, saying, My name is Legion: for we are many* [Mark 5:6–9].

There were a legion of evil spirits in him.

> *When the unclean spirit is gone out of a man, he walketh* (goes) *through dry places, seeking rest, and findeth none.*
> *Then he saith, I will return into my house from whence I came out; and when he is come, he findeth it empty, swept, and garnished* (put in order).
> *Then goeth he, and taketh with himself seven other spirits more wicked than himself, and they enter in and dwell there: and the last state of that man is worse than the first. Even so shall it be also unto this wicked generation* [Matt. 12:43–45].

There are several evil spirits. But there is only one Holy Spirit. He is the One functioning in the community of believers and creating unity. The Holy Spirit is not only an influence on the community of believers, the Church as we know it, but He is the One maintaining it and operating within it. He is One person, indivisible, as are the Father and Son.

The Holy Spirit will do certain things, *when He shall come* as our Lord says. What are some of the things the Holy Spirit will do or is doing?

First, He always does essentially the same work. Because He does, there is an essential unity among the community of believers. Note that I said essentially the same. I did not say exactly the same. No two flowers of the same species and color are 100 percent identical.

Man is accustomed to mass production and working in a mechanical manner. We have been brainwashed into thinking everyone should do everything the same way.

The Holy Spirit works within the community and among the individual members. The Holy Spirit's work, being essentially the same, means that it is always a living, vital work, not mechanical and identical.

Second, the Holy Spirit prepares us so that we can become members of the community of believers. Paul amplifies upon this, saying,

> *In whom all the building fitly framed* (being joined) *together groweth unto a holy temple in the Lord* [Eph. 2:21].

Remember, we discussed preparing the stones with hammers and chisels, shaping them, rubbing them, polishing them, and fitting them in the proper place.

The Holy Spirit has much to do with the natural person before he or she can become an effective member of the body of Christ. This poignant fact needs to be realized and remembered. Unless we do so we will experience unnecessary problems within the community.

Third, the Holy Spirit makes it possible for us to become members of the invisible church, the body of Christ, by preparing us beforehand. You may become a member of the visible church in various ways, family, friends, marriage, community, or whatever. As we are by nature (the natural man), we cannot be part of the Lord in all His glory and purity.

> *Know ye not that the unrighteous shall not inherit the kingdom of God? Be not deceived: neither fornicators* (the sexually immoral), *nor idolaters, nor adulterers, nor effeminate* (homosexuals), *nor abusers* (sodomites) *of themselves with mankind,*
> *Nor thieves, nor covetous, nor drunkards, nor revilers, nor extortioners, shall inherit the kingdom of God. And such were some of you: but ye are washed, but ye are sanctified* (set apart), *but ye are justified* (declared righteous) *in the name of the Lord Jesus, and by the Spirit of our God* [1 Cor. 6:9–11].
>
> Note, we are justified and sanctified by . . . *the name of the Lord Jesus, and by the Spirit of our God* [1 Cor. 6:11].

We need the Holy Spirit working within us.

Calvin provides additional clarity to Paul's words as he expounds upon them declaring, "By unrighteousness we are to understand what is opposed to strict morality. So it is that those who cause injury to their brothers, who cheat and defraud others, who, in a word trample on others in the pursuit of their own interests, are the unrighteous who will not enter into possession of the kingdom of God. It is too obvious for words that here when Paul gives instances of unrighteousness people, . . . he means those who do not repent of their sins, but obstinately persist in them.

"The meaning therefore is simply this: before they had received the grace of regeneration some of the Corinthians (and those ever since) were covetous, others adulterers, others extortioners, others effeminate, others revilers; but now having truly been set free by Christ they were like that no longer.

"Paul makes a prayer and judicious distinction between functions. For the blood of Christ is the cause of our cleansing; from His death and resurrection we obtain righteousness and sanctification. But since the cleansing which Christ has carried out and the obtaining of righteousness are of no benefit to any except those who have been made to share in those blessings by the power of the Holy Spirit, Paul is quite right in speaking of the Spirit along with Christ. Christ, therefore, is the source of every blessing to us; it is from Him that we obtain everything. But Christ Himself, with all His blessings, is communicated to us by the Spirit. For we receive Christ by faith; and it is by faith that His benefits (*gratiae*) are applied to us. The author of faith is the Spirit."

Fourth, the Holy Spirit produces unity. Divisions occur primarily within individual congregations or among denominations because other matters or elements are accounted more important than the work of the Holy Spirit, and being members of the body of Christ.

The churches, as we know them, are to a great extent based upon and governed by either man-made traditions or mindsets developed by experience. Therefore, divisions persist because people do not realize or accept the fact that apart from the Holy Spirit there is no true church. It does not matter what the appearances may be.

We have considered a few things that the Holy Spirit does or is in the process of doing. However, there are other questions to explore. What is the work of the Holy Spirit? How does it impact upon us as members of the community of believers?

When considering these important questions, it is proper to digress for a moment and consider the Doctrine of the Holy Spirit and the expression of it since the time Christ dwelled on earth.

Yes, the Holy Spirit was presented by our Lord in His teachings. The apostles wrote about the Holy Spirit in the Gospels and the Epistles. The Holy Spirit is identified in the Apostles' Creed. We accept the Doctrine of the Holy Trinity. The theologians and scholars of the Middle Ages dealt with the Holy Spirit in diverse ways and manners.

Then Calvin came upon the scene and began to grapple and wrestle with some of these questions. It was obvious that the Holy Spirit as presented in the New Testament could not be dealt with exclusively within the Doctrine of the Trinity. Calvin propounded Augustine's theology of the Trinity with increasing clarity and comprehensiveness. Also, he devoted time and thought to the Holy Spirit.

It is interesting to note the titles of the four books in Calvin's last version of his Institutes. According to Calvin they are structured to conform to the four parts of the Apostles' Creed. Please note the titles of the four books,

- *The Knowledge of God the Creator*;
- *The Knowledge of God the Redeemer*;
- *The Way in Which We Receive the Grace of Christ*; and
- *The External Means or Aids by Which God Invites Us Into the Society of Christ and Holds us Therein*.

There is no mention of the Holy Spirit in these titles. Apparently, Calvin did not think it was possible to present the work of the Spirit in the same manner as God the Creator and God the Redeemer. Book 3 begins with an outline of the Spirit. What follows is just as much in the Spirit, as Calvin presents expository teachings concerning faith, repentance, life of the Christian, justification, Christian freedom, and election and the Resurrection. Calvin continues to present the Spirit in Book 4. He distinguishes between believing in the Spirit and faithful membership in the church.

Further, in discussing the sacraments Calvin presents the person of the Holy Spirit. Why present this material? It is important to note that Calvin gave up his initial order and structure when he encountered the Holy Spirit. To Calvin, the Spirit was in the creation. Also, He was and is with Christ.

Whatever can be said about faith, repentance, redemption, the Christian life, justification, and even the sacraments involves the Spirit. Wherever you turn with respect to God and to Jesus Christ you find the Holy Spirit.

"The Spirit is not the Creator, nor is He the reconciler, but in Him God shows Himself to be the creator and the reconciler in that He "sanctifies" us, that is, claims us for Himself and thus removes us from our power of disposal over ourselves," as described with clarity and emphasis by Otto Weber.

The Holy Spirit demonstrates that God is the Creator and the Reconciler. Further, He appropriates to us the work of Jesus Christ. The Holy Spirit is alive in the work of Christ. The work of the Spirit is evidenced in three ways: attesting to the witness of Jesus Christ, making effective the reconciliation Jesus has fashioned for us, and realizing Christ's royal kingship. The Barmen Declaration of 1934 states "Jesus Christ as attested to us in Holy Scripture is the one word of God whom we must hear and whom we must trust and obey in life and in death."

He (Christ) is both the Reconciler and the Revealer. He turns to us, we do not turn to Him. He comes to us in the Word, which He is, and in the Word, which He speaks. The Spirit does not cause this to happen.

Jesus is the witness to the Father. This is revealed in John's Gospel when Jesus says, *For I have not spoken of myself* (my own authority); *but the Father which sent me, he gave me a commandment, what I should say and what I should speak* [John 12:49].

It is by the work of the Spirit in us that we know these teachings to be true. It is in the Spirit that Christ comes toward us. And it is the Spirit that witnesses to the Son and to those belonging to the Son.

The Doctrine of the Holy Spirit depends not only on experiences verified by their fruit in the lives of the members of the community, but also is based on the fact that Christ died and is alive again. *For Christ also hath once suffered for sins, the just for the unjust, that he might bring us to God, being put to death in the flesh, but quickened* (made alive) *by the Spirit* [1 Pet. 3:18]. The Spirit is known both as God's gracious power and as the presence of Christ Himself.

The question may be asked: did Jesus attest to Himself? Yes, He did. Jesus received the Spirit as stated in Scripture,

> *THEN was Jesus led up of the spirit into the wilderness to be tempted of the devil* [Matt. 4:1].
>
> *AND Jesus being full of the Holy Ghost* (Holy Spirit) *returned from Jordan, and was led by the Spirit into the wilderness* [Luke 4:1].

He subjects Himself to the Father as the obedient One.

The glory of the Father is manifest in the Son's obedience.

> *And Jesus answering said unto him, Suffer* (allow) *it to be so now: for thus it becometh* (is fitting for) *us to fulfill all righteousness. Then he suffered* (allowed) *him.*

> *And Jesus, when he was baptized, went up straightway out of the water: and, lo, the heavens were opened unto him, and he saw the Spirit of God descending like a dove, and lighting upon him:*
>
> *And lo a voice from heaven, saying, This is my beloved Son, in whom I am well pleased* [Matt. 3:15–17].

Jesus makes a profound, illuminating statement, saying, . . . *the words that I speak unto you, they are spirit, and they are life* [John 6:63]. His words are effective and express His faith. The Spirit also attests to Jesus. Please note the truths proclaimed regarding the Holy Spirit. John records that Jesus also said,

> *But the Comforter* (Paraclete), *which is the Holy Ghost, whom the Father will send in my name, he shall teach you all things, and bring all things to your remembrance, whatsoever I have said unto you* [John 14:26].
>
> *Howbeit when he, the Spirit of truth, is come, he will guide you into all truth: for he shall not speak of himself* (on his own authority); *but whatsoever he shall hear, that shall he speak* [John 16:13].

In addition, Paul writing to Timothy tells him

> *That good thing which was committed unto thee keep by the Holy Ghost which dwelleth in us* [2 Tim. 1:14].

The Word based in the Spirit is shown through the Spirit to be true and valid. The present day witness to Jesus Christ in word and in deed depends upon the Holy Spirit.

Some interpret it as people affecting people and take it as a form of persuasion. However, in truth it is the witness of the Holy Spirit. The power, the impact, is due to the Holy Spirit, and it can occur where there appears to be only weakness. It is empowered through the Lord who is the Spirit.

The person believing in the power and work of the Holy Spirit is able to proclaim the Word with humility and authority. Christ manifests Himself to the community through the Spirit.

When was the Spirit given? And the apostles *being assembled together* after the resurrection were *commanded* by Jesus to *wait for the promise of the Father, which . . . ye have heard of me. . . . But ye shall receive power, after* (when) *that the Holy Ghost is come upon you* [Acts 1:4–8].

Then, on Pentecost day, when the apostles were gathered together *they were all filled with the Holy Ghost* [Acts 2:4]. The Lord's promise was fulfilled at Pentecost. On that day, the church was constituted as a reality, and its growth began.

Luke records in the Book of Acts what the members of the early church did. Note the four things the people did after being converted. They applied themselves to strengthening their faith by (i) hearing the apostles doctrine, that which the Son of God had delivered to them; (ii) breaking bread together, which Calvin believes was celebrating the Lord's Supper; (iii) having fellowship with one another within the community of believers; and (iv) gathering together for public prayers. This was how the early believers professed their faith and grew in it.

Most of us are familiar with the account in Acts. However, when thinking of the Holy Spirit we should also consider John enlightening us with the following:

> *Then the same day at evening, being the first day of the week, when the doors were shut where the disciples were assembled for fear of the Jews, came Jesus and stood in the midst, and saith unto them, Peace be unto you.*
>
> *And when he had so said, he showed unto them his hands and his side. Then were the disciples glad, when they saw the Lord.*
>
> *Then said Jesus to them again, Peace be unto you: as my Father hath sent me, even so send I you.*
>
> *And when he had said this, he breathed on them, and saith unto them, Receive ye the Holy Ghost:*
>
> *Whosesoever sins ye remit* (forgive), *they are remitted* (forgiven) *unto them; and whosesoever sins ye retain, they are retained* [John 20:19–23].

Jesus breathed on the assembled disciples and said, *Receive ye the Holy Ghost.*

The Holy Ghost was to guide them, work with them, and provide them with power. May He do the same with us today.

Amen!

7

The Holy Spirit

> *There is one body, and one Spirit, even as ye are called in one hope of your calling;*
> *One Lord, one faith, one baptism,*
> *One God and Father of all, who is above all, and through all, and in you all* [Eph. 4:4–6].

Jesus said to the gathered disciples, *Receive ye the Holy Ghost* [John 20:22]. Pentecost was the occasion when the whole body of disciples plus others had this overwhelming experience. However, theologically and sequentially John correctly provides emphasis on the Holy Spirit by recording Jesus' words that the Father

> *. . . shall give you another Comforter* (Paraclete*)*
> *. . . whom the world cannot receive, because it seeth him not, . . . but ye know him; for he dwelleth with you, and shall be in you* [John 14:16–17].
>
> *But when the Comforter* (Helper) *is come, . . . he shall testify of me* [John 15:26].

The resurrection appearance made Peter a new man as well as each of the other ten disciples. It may have been several weeks before the larger community was joined into one faith and heart, thus making possible the Pentecostal event recorded in the second chapter of Acts. Note Luke's words in Acts,

> *While Peter yet spake these words, the Holy Ghost fell on all them which heard the word.*
>
> *And they* (the Jews) *of the circumcision which believed were astonished, as many as came with Peter, because that on the Gentiles also was poured out the gift of the Holy Ghost.*
>
> *For they heard them speak with tongues, and magnify God. Then answered Peter,*
>
> *Can any man forbid water, that these should not be baptized, which have received the Holy Ghost as well as we?*
>
> *And he commanded them to be baptized in the name of the Lord. Then prayed* (asked) *they him to tarry* (stay) *certain days* [Acts 10:44–48].

This is referred to by some as the "Gentile Pentecost."

Dr. R. Newton Flew points out that among the early believers the following truths were accepted, after the giving and the receiving of the Holy Spirit, stating there was

> *"A conviction that the living God was at work;*
> *the Spirit was received by all Christians; and*
> > *the Spirit was not a private possession of one person, or small group, but was shared by the whole community."*

Therefore, the church was established as a new reality with the members rejoicing and thanking God for reconciling them through the Lord Jesus Christ.

God's reconciling act in Jesus Christ is made concrete through the Spirit. It confronts and draws a person in this world. Certain developments occur as a result of being reconciled with God.

First, the Holy Spirit convicts us of sin. By nature we are satisfied with ourselves. We may not be satisfied with others, whether they be members of our family or not, but people are usually satisfied with themselves.

Consider what Christ says of the Comforter,

> *And when he is come, he will reprove* (convict) *the world of sin, and of righteousness, and of judgment* [John 16:8].

Reprove in this verse means "convict." The Greek word is *elegcho*.

The Holy Spirit enables us to realize the truth concerning God's holiness. We do not know much about this until the Holy Spirit begins to work within us. When you think about it, two things occur about the same time: we become convicted of our sin; and we learn about the holiness of God. Ponder that!

The Holy Spirit awakens us to the sin that dwells within, and to the holy nature of God. Isaac Watts says it beautifully in When I Survey the Wondrous Cross.

> *When I survey the wondrous cross*
> *On which the Prince of Glory died,*
> *My richest gain I count but loss,*
> *And pour contempt on all my pride.*
>
> *Forbid it Lord, that I should boast,*
> *Save in the death of Christ my God,*
> *All the vain things that charm me most,*
> *I sacrifice them to His blood.*
>
> *See, from His head, His hands, His feet,*
> *Sorrow and love flow mingled down:*
> *Did e'er such love and sorrow meet,*
> *Or thorns compose so rich a crown?*
>
> *Were the whole realm of nature mine,*
> *That were a present far too small;*
> *Love so amazing, so divine,*
> *Demands my soul, my life, my all."*

Charles Wesley expresses it with beauty, humility, and simplicity, saying,

> "Just and holy is thy name,
> I am all unrighteousness;
> False and full of sin I am,
> Thou art full of truth and grace."

Our first great need is to be brought down, to be humbled and humiliated. This is the first work of the Holy Spirit.

The second development is quickening and regeneration, which results in a new principle of life. You cannot be a member of the body of Christ without having His life in you. This must happen; it is a necessity. We must be remade from the very beginning, or from the basic foundation. The Apostle says,

> AND you hath He quickened (made alive), who were dead in trespasses and sins [Eph. 2:1].

The member of Christ's body is a partaker of the divine nature and a member of the household of God. The result of the quickening and regeneration is that a person is able to exercise faith and to have a measure of understanding. This special work of the Holy Spirit is to glorify the Lord Jesus Christ.

Third, the reconciling work of Jesus Christ is peace. What does this mean? That in Jesus Christ and by virtue of what He has done and suffered, everything between man and God is "in tune," or in a right relationship. Nothing else is required and it is unconditional. Paul states with clarity and understanding, *THEREFORE being justified by faith, we have peace with God through our Lord Jesus Christ* [Rom. 5:1]. God has left nothing undone, nor has He done anything halfway.

Through Christ's reconciling activity we have life which is the exact opposite to enmity and death. Paul says to the Romans and Ephesians,

> *For to be carnally minded is death; but to be spiritually minded is life and peace* [Rom. 8:6].
>
> *For if, when we were enemies, we were reconciled to God by the death of His Son, much more, being* (having been) *reconciled, we shall be saved by His life* [Rom. 5:10].
>
> *For he* (himself) *is our peace, who hath made both one, and hath broken down the middle wall of partition* (division) *between us* [Eph. 2:14].

An excellent summary of this is found in Romans, which says,

> *For the kingdom of God is not meat* (food) *and drink; but righteousness, and peace, and joy in the Holy Ghost* [Rom. 14:17].

This reconciling peace is the peace of God which surpasseth all understanding. It is the Spirit that makes this peace of God a reality in us and among us.

John Calvin amplifies on these penetrating words of Paul's stating that he "has not contrasted these with food and drink . . . for the purpose of enumerating all that constitutes the kingdom of Christ, but of showing that it consists of spiritual things. He has, however, summed up in a few words all that the gospel means, viz. consciousness of moral goodness, peace with God, and the possession of true joy of conscience through the Holy Spirit dwelling in us. As I have said, he has applied these few attributes to his present argument . . . . What more do those who have peace with God desire? "By connecting peace with joy, he is expressing . . . the mode of this spiritual joy, for however listless or buoyed up the reprobate may be, the conscience is made glad and cheerful only when it feels God to be reconciled and favorable to it. Only this peace provides true joy. Although it was in Paul's interest to declare, when he mentioned these great gifts, that the Spirit was the author of them, in this passage he wanted to suggest the contrast which existed between the spirit and outward blessings, so that we should know that we may enjoy all the gifts which belong to the kingdom of God without the use of food."

There is a contemporary belief that there is such a thing as "peace of the conscience." However, when examining Scripture, we find this is not the case. *For God is not the author of confusion* (disorder), *but of peace, as in all churches of the saints* [1 Cor. 14:33]. The context of this statement is man's relationship to his fellow man. Man's inward state or condition takes a back seat in importance with respect to the community. The New Testament never speaks about the peace of conscience. If the community is reconciled, then all enmity is at an end . . . *we both have access by one Spirit unto the Father* [Eph. 2:18].

Reconciliation occurs and peace is created where once there was enmity. The teaching of our Lord is rather explicit:

> *Ye have heard that it hath been said, THOU SHALT LOVE THY NEIGHBOR, and hate thine enemy.*
> *But I say unto you, Love your enemies, bless them that curse you, do good to them that hate you, and pray for them which despitefully* (spitefully) *use you, and persecute you;*
> *That ye may be the children* (sons) *of your Father which is in heaven: for he maketh his sun to rise on the evil and on the good, and sendeth rain on the just and on the unjust.*
> *For if ye love them which love you, what reward have ye? do not even the publicans* (tax collectors) *the same?*
> *And if ye salute* (greet) *your brethren only, what do ye more than others? do not even the publicans* (tax collectors) *so?*
> *Be ye therefore perfect, even as your Father which is in heaven is perfect* [Matt. 5:43–48].
>
> *Bless them which persecute you: bless, and curse not*
> [Rom. 12:14].

The peace established by God in Jesus Christ is not restricted to a person's inward state. It extends to interpersonal relationships. The body of Christ is the place of peace. The New Testament stresses the lack of peace and the damage it inflicts. The lusts of the flesh and mind produce conflict and disharmony, not peace. Paul says to the Galatians,

> *But if ye bite and devour one another, take heed that ye be not consumed one of another.*
> *This I say then, Walk in the Spirit, and ye shall not fulfill the lust of the flesh* [Gal. 5:15–16].

There can be no serious talk of peace with God where the community is marked by a lack of peace. Where there is peace with God the fruit of the Spirit emerges, and it is manifested in the community as it witnesses to those far and near.

Fourth, what impact does the Spirit have on our relationship to God as we realize reconciliation? The Spirit affects "sonship" or adoption. Paul speaks to the Romans and the Galatians regarding their adoption and being *an heir of God*,

> *For ye have not received the spirit of bondage again to fear; but ye have received the Spirit of adoption, whereby we cry, Abba, Father* [Rom. 8:15].

> *To redeem them that were under the law, that we might receive the adoption of sons.*
> *And because ye are sons, God hath sent forth the Spirit of his Son into your hearts, crying, Abba, Father.*
> *Wherefore thou art no more a servant, but a son; and if a son, then an heir of God through Christ*
> [Gal. 4:5–7].

This "sonship" or adoption means being heirs and having freedom *in Christ*.

However, please note that the New Testament does not express or infer anywhere that sonship or adoption belongs to man, sinful man, in and of himself. This is important. When Jesus called God "Father," He was going back to what the Old Testament expressed. Who is Yahweh? He is the Father of the covenant people. Jesus proclaims that the Father receives back to Himself the runaway children.

Why stress this point? Because the New Testament teaching has been harmed and distorted by the rather abstract and general declaration of a false thesis that God is in reality or fact the Father of all, and that all people regardless of their condition are His children.

Even with regard to baptism, we become God's children under certain conditions and remain true to the Bible. Baptism should not be separated from the Spirit and from faith.

Adoption is the gift of Christ, and it is real for us in the Holy Spirit. Adoption is an element of reconciliation, and that is how it was looked upon in the older theology.

God did not make peace with man once and only once, but He made peace once and for all. Thus the believer should know that he is "in tune" with God, not only today but forever. He should know that Christ intercedes for Him.

> *AND the third day there was a marriage in Cana of Galilee; and the mother of Jesus was there:*
> *And both Jesus was called* (invited), *and his disciples, to the marriage* [John 2:1–2].
>
> *Wherefore he is able also to save them to the uttermost that come unto God by him, seeing he ever liveth to make intercession for them* [Heb. 7:25].
>
> *Who is he that condemneth? It is Christ that died, yea rather, that is risen again, who is even at the right hand of God, who also maketh intercession for us* [Rom. 8:34].

We need to grasp the fact that believers never stand before God by themselves. They are not dependent upon their own actions but upon Christ, the Intercessor.

The nature of man reveals the following: adoption means we are on God's side, which is contrary to human nature; and intercession means that God in Christ is on our side today, tomorrow, and forever, despite everything that is true regarding the natural man. Paul says to the Romans,

> *Likewise the Spirit also helpeth our infirmities* (weaknesses): *for we know not what we should pray for as we ought: but the Spirit itself maketh intercession for us with groanings which cannot be uttered.*
> *And he that searcheth the hearts knoweth what is the mind of the Spirit, because he maketh intercession for the saints according to the will of God.*
> *And we know that all things work together for good to them that love God, to them who are the called according to his purpose.*

> *For whom he did foreknow, he also did predestinate to be conformed to the image of his Son, that he might be the first-born among many brethren.*
>
> *Moreover whom he did predestinate, them he also called: and whom he called, them he also justified: and whom he justified, them he also glorified* [Rom. 8:26–30].

The believer is not by himself or herself; God is with them, and He is with us.

The fifth development which occurs from being reconciled with God is realizing Christ's kingly office. Calvin discussed Christ's kingly office with resolve. He thought it impossible to see the office of Christ solely in His death, and that Christ's death was not the ultimate achievement of His objective but only part of it, which included establishing His kingdom. Jesus' work and life were for our benefit, including God making peace with us, individually. His objectives include a new creation, establishing His kingdom, and Christ's kingship.

> *Jesus answered, My kingdom is not of this world: if my kingdom were of this world, then would my servants fight, that I should not be delivered to the Jews: but now is my kingdom not from hence.*
>
> *Pilate therefore said unto him, Art thou a king then? Jesus answered, Thou sayest* (rightly) *that I am a king. To this end was I born, and for this cause came I into the world, that I should bear witness unto the truth. Every one that is of the truth heareth my voice* [John 18:36–37].
>
> *And I appoint* (bestow upon) *unto you a kingdom, as my Father hath appointed unto* (bestowed upon) *me;*
>
> *That ye may eat and drink at my table in my kingdom, and sit on thrones judging the twelve tribes of Israel* [Luke 22:29–30].

It is important to consider the next step by which the Holy Spirit incorporates us into the body of Christ as He unites us to Him. As a result, we are united to one another.

> *For by one Spirit are we all baptized into one body, whether we be Jews or Gentiles* (Greeks), *whether we be bond* (slaves) *or free; and have been all made to drink into one Spirit* [1 Cor. 12:13].

It is the Spirit who baptizes us into the body of Christ.

There are two portions of Scripture to consider:

> *Know ye not that ye are the temple of God, and that the Spirit of God dwelleth in you?*
>
> *If any man defile* (destroys) *the temple of God, him shall God destroy; for the temple of God is holy, which temple ye are* [1 Cor. 3:16–17].

> *What? know ye not that your body is the temple of the Holy Ghost which is in you, which ye have of God, and ye are not your own?*
>
> *For ye are bought with a price: therefore glorify God in your body, and in your spirit, which are God's* [1 Cor. 6:19–20].

In the former, Paul through the Holy Spirit is speaking about the church or community of believers, whereas in the latter he is addressing individuals.

Calvin speaks in a straightforward manner when he elaborates on Paul's statements to the Corinthians (and us) regarding our bodies being *the temple of the Holy Ghost*, being *bought with a price*, and that we are to *glorify God*. He states that "Paul uses two further arguments to keep us away from this filthiness. The first is that 'our bodies are temples of the spirit' and the second that we are not under our own jurisdiction because the Lord has acquired us for Himself as His own private property . . . . we make ourselves His dwelling-place only by consecrating ourselves as His temples. What a great honor God bestows upon us in wishing to dwell in us.

"This is the second argument, viz. that we are not under our own authority to live as we want. The reason he gives for that is that the Lord has paid the price for our redemption, and acquired us for Himself . . . 'For Christ died and rose, in order He might be the Lord of the living and the dead.'

"Glorify God . . . From this conclusion it is plain that the Corinthians assumed that they could do what they pleased in regard to external matters and that had to be checked and bridled. Paul . . . warns them that the body, just as much as the soul, is subject to God, and therefore it is only right that both should serve His glory. . . . 'Indeed the mind of a believer must be pure before God, but also the outward conduct, which men see, must be in conformity, seeing that authority over both belongs to God, who has redeemed both' . . . not only our souls, but also our bodies are temples of the Holy Spirit, so that we may be under no delusion about acquitting ourselves well towards Him, for we can only do that when we yield ourselves to His service, wholly and completely, so that He may also direct the outward actions of our lives by His Word."

The Holy Spirit works within us. We do not do it by ourselves. Why does He do this work? So we can become more and more like Jesus Christ. John says,

> Beloved, now are we the sons (children) of God, and it doth not yet appear what we shall be: but we know that, when he shall appear, we shall be like him; for we shall see him as he is [1 John 3:2].

The work of the Holy Spirit produces the same fruit in us when He dwells within us. He dwells within the community and within each individual. What fruit does He produce?

> ... the fruit of the spirit is love, joy, peace, long-suffering, gentleness (kindness), goodness, faith (faithfulness),
> Meekness, temperance (self-control) [Gal. 5:22–23].

This is true of the members of Christ's body wherever they may be and of whatever nationality. It is the Spirit that produces this fruit. We do not. When the Spirit produces this fruit, there is unity in the community.

What prevents the unity from developing is our natural condition, self-centeredness, and all those traits that derive from self, including self-importance, self-interests, and self-rationalizations.

When you become joined to the body of Christ, you do not lose your personality in a basic sense, but you are no longer governed by it. Your personality becomes governed by the Holy Spirit, and as a result, the various graces of the fruit of the Spirit begin to shine forth. We all love to see this fruit appear in other people, and pray God that this fruit will be so abundant in us that nothing else can be seen.

The lusts of the flesh divide. The fruit of the Spirit unites. It is easy to understand that the lusts of the flesh divide. We have all seen the results of the suffering, remorse, and callousness that they produce. Paul speaks forthrightly, saying,

> Now the works of the flesh are manifest (evident), which are these; adultery, fornication, uncleanness, lasciviousness (licentiousness),
> Idolatry, witchcraft (sorcery), hatred, variance (contentions), emulations, wrath, strife (selfish ambitions), seditions (dissensions), heresies,

> *Envyings, murders, drunkenness, revellings, and such like: of the which I tell you before, as I have also told you in time past, that they which do such things shall not inherit the kingdom of God* [Gal. 5:19–21].

On the other hand, the fruit of the Spirit is different. It is the work of the Holy Spirit that brings together family and friends. It strengthens the tie that binds them together. The words that describe the fruit of the Spirit are uplifting and melodious. Hear the words of Paul ringing out to us,

> *But the fruit of the Spirit is love, joy, peace, long-suffering, gentleness* (kindness), *goodness, faith* (faithfulness),
> *Meekness, temperance* (self-control): *against such there is no law* [Gal. 5:22–23].

We are to practice these traits. Pray God He will send the Holy Spirit to strengthen us, and to rebuke us if necessary.

When the Holy Spirit produces this fruit there is no room left for discord or division.

There is a dilemma when considering the Holy Spirit and His work within us. This dilemma consists of the fact that the Spirit does not overwhelm us or overpower us, nor does He leave us with our own imagined autonomy. He does not make and force every decision upon us, but He gives us the freedom and strength to do the will of God.

The questions as to what we are able to do or unable to do in matters of faith have been decided already. Those who discuss this point endlessly are the ones who do not believe.

People may insist upon their power of decision-making. They may appeal to their experiences, their mindset, their philosophy. Those people are characterized by focusing upon: what they are; what they have in and of themselves; and what they think. Though they think they have freedom, it is in reality a usurped autonomy which man has asserted for himself. It is apart from God's activity.

This assertion is a closed mind or as Weber says a "closedness." It is an incapacity or attitude by which a person or group does not allow God's word or the work of the Holy Spirit to be valid.

The dilemma of which we spoke earlier has a very practical application for the believer or member of the community.

- How do I have the ability or freedom to be or to become something that I am not, based upon my experience?
- How can I do that which I cannot truly do on my own and for the most part do not even want to do?
- How do I realize the freedom or desire to do these things although they may not be part of the habit within me?

These questions need to be asked, especially when considering the one Spirit.

How do these things happen? Not by our own control, wills, or condition. They occur because the revealed reality of God is greater than our hearts. John says, *For if our heart condemn us, God is greater than our heart, and knoweth all things* [1 John 3:20]. Further, the Apostle says,

> *Beloved, if our heart condemn us not, then have we confidence toward God.*
>
> *And whatsoever we ask, we receive of him, because we keep his commandments, and do those things that are pleasing in his sight.*
>
> *And this is his commandment, That we should believe on the name of his Son Jesus Christ, and love one another, as he gave us commandment.*
>
> *And he that keepeth his commandments dwelleth in him, and he in him. And hereby we know that he abideth in us, by the Spirit which he hath given us* [1 John 3:21–24].

When asking these questions a certain light should dawn upon us. Our lack of ability or understanding is not based upon our inherent capabilities or knowledge, but because of our enmity toward God's grace, and our closed minds. But thank God that He is not closed. Rather, He is the revealer and reconciler in our Lord Jesus Christ.

God emerges when His Word encounters us and by one Spirit is able to draw us out of ourselves and to grasp us. Why? So we can grasp this reality ourselves. The reality is Jesus Christ, the living Lord. He is alive and real in the Word, which is fashioned by the one Spirit and made effective by the one Spirit.

The way we grasp the Word and the living Christ is described by Paul in his letter to the Philippians,

> *Not as though I had already attained, . . .*
> *. . . but this one thing I do, . . .*

> *I press toward the mark for the prize of the high calling of God in Christ Jesus* [Phil. 3:12–14].

Whenever the Spirit works in us, we become active in receiving, rich in our poverty, and powerful in our weakness.

Remember what the Lord Jesus told Paul,

> *For this thing I besought* (pleaded with) *the Lord thrice* (three times), *that it might depart from me.*
>
> *And he said unto me, My grace is sufficient for thee: for my strength* (power) *is made perfect in weakness. Most gladly therefore will I rather glory in my infirmities* (weaknesses), *that the power of Christ may rest upon me.*
>
> *Therefore I take pleasure in infirmities, in reproaches, in necessities, in persecutions, in distresses for Christ's sake: for when I am weak, then am I strong.*
>
> *I am become a fool in glorying* (boasting); *ye have compelled me: for I ought to have been commended of you: for in nothing am I behind the very chiefest apostles, though I be nothing.*
>
> *Truly the signs of an apostle were wrought among you in all patience* (perseverance), *in signs, and wonders, and mighty deeds* [2 Cor. 12:8–12].

Thanks be to God for His Word, His Spirit, and His Son. *Amen.*

8

Looking Forward

> *There is one body, and one Spirit, even as ye are called in one hope of your calling* [Eph. 4:4].

The Apostle Paul is desirous, even anxious, for the Ephesians to know more about our Lord Jesus Christ and to draw closer to Him. Therefore, the Apostle presents and amplifies upon the Holy Spirit. Why? Because it is the Spirit that reveals the Son more fully and bears witness to Him.

> *There is one body, and one spirit, even as ye are called in one hope of your calling* [Eph. 4:4].

Please note the sequence: one body, the life of the body, and the power that keeps it alive and enables it to act is the one Spirit.

The Apostle, in this verse and the following two, emphasizes the word *one* and the term "unity." A question to ponder: Why did the Apostle add the phrase *even as ye are called in one hope of your calling*? Paul wrote with forethought and care. He was logical in his presentations to the community of believers.

Therefore, Paul specifically states, *as ye are called in one hope of your calling*. He wanted them to understand why the Holy Spirit acted as He did regarding those who are called, and what actually happened: He effectually called them; He *quickened* them, which means in Greek "to give life together" or "to preserve life together," those who were dead in their trespasses and sins; He convicted them of sin and enabled them to learn about the holiness of God; He gave them a new life; and He baptized them into the body of Christ. These things happened in preparing them for something that had not happened, something that was going to happen.

There is an important point to consider. The Church is not an end in and of itself, even though many people consider it in this way.

What is the church or the community of believers? Or better yet, what is "the Church" supposed to be? It is supposed to be the body of Christ. It is the instrument by which God and the Holy Spirit call people to be a new people, a people obedient to the will of God. Therefore, you have the sequence *one body, one spirit*, and *one hope*.

The Apostle reminds the Ephesians that he is praying for them that the eyes of their understanding may be enlightened, they may know the hope of their calling, the riches of the glory of His inheritance in the saints, and the exceeding greatness of His power that is given to us who believe.

By doing this, the Apostle develops and emphasizes the principle of unity. He appeals to the followers *to keep the unity of the Spirit in the bond of peace* [Eph. 4:3]. What promotes unity? What guards it? What keeps it?

> . . . *ye are called in one hope of your calling* [Eph. 4:4].

When you fail to keep our eye on *the hope of your calling,* what happens? Divisions, distinctions, and misunderstandings not only develop, but continue to exist.

This happens in numerous ways. First, people dwell upon what they have been called from rather than dwelling on to what they have been called. We have been called to God's side to . . . *walk worthy of the vocation* (calling) *wherewith ye are called* [Eph. 4:1].

Second, there is a tendency to look back, to talk about it, and to extol it. This causes distinctions and divisions. It is in this way that Satan creates trouble and causes damage. He causes people to look backwards instead of looking to what they have been called. That was evident in the early church, in the distinctions of Jew–Gentile, barbarian–Scythian, bond–free, male–female. When these distinctions or former divisions are perpetuated among the community of believers, then divisions fester and widen.

Third, this happens in a very subtle way. It occurs when people relate their experiences *in Christ* or how they came to know Him. Perhaps an illustration by Martyn Lloyd-Jones will help.

"A man gave his testimony as to how he came to know and accept Christ. He described how terrible he had been, yet despite his dreadful sinfulness, God had laid hold of him and converted him.

"When he finished another man stepped forward to tell of his conversion. He started by saying, you have heard so-and-so tell his story. Well, I want to tell you he does not know what sin is. I will tell you how bad it really was. Then he launched into a lurid description of his past. He was trying to outdo the other person.

"He was boasting of his sinfulness; he was drawing a distinction, creating a division. He wanted to prove that his conversion was the greater one.

"That approach is wrong and unscriptural! All conversions are identical in the ultimate sense. *They occur by the grace and power of Almighty God.* Your background, nationality, family, wealth, ability, or anything else does not matter." Paul says,

> *For by grace are ye* (have been) *saved through faith; and that not of yourselves: it is the gift of God:*
> *Not of works, lest any man should boast* [Eph. 2:8–9].

As Paul says, we are not to look at what we have been saved from, but to what we are saved by God's grace.

Fourth, the conversion experience, or the way we come to know Christ, is not the important thing, nor is it something to cause divisions or distinctions. The important matter is that God by His grace has called us and you *are called in one hope of your calling* [Eph. 4:4].

This point is illustrated by John McNeil, a minister in Scotland, and was related by Martyn Lloyd-Jones. Reverend McNeil preached a sermon in which he drew a comparison between the blind man who received his sight as recounted in the Gospels of both Mark and John. It is recorded in John's Gospel that

> *And his disciples asked him* (Jesus), . . . *who did sin, this man, or his parents, that he was born blind* [John 9:2]?
>
> . . . *he spat upon the ground, and made clay of the spittle* (saliva), *and he anointed* (applied the clay upon) *the eyes of the blind man with the clay,*
> *And said unto him, Go, wash in the pool of Siloam,* . . . *He went his way therefore, and washed, and came seeing* [John 9:6–7].

In Mark's Gospel, when Jesus was in Bethsaida they brought a blind man to him

> *And he took the blind man by the hand, and led him out of the town; and when he had spit on his eyes, and put his hands upon him, he asked him if he saw ought* (anything).
> *And he looked up, and said, I see men as trees, walking.*
> *After that he put his hands again upon his eyes, and made him look up: and he was restored, and saw every man clearly* [Mark 8:23–25].

McNeil, in his sermon, imagined that at some later time these two men met and discussed what happened and how they received their sight.

The man from John said, "What did it feel like when He put the mixture of spittle and clay on your eyes"?

The man from Mark asked, "Spittle and clay mixture? I do not know anything about that."

The man from John said, "What? You mean you do not remember how Jesus spat on the ground, made a mixture, and then applied it to your eyes? What did it feel like when He applied it to your eyes?"

The man in Mark said, "He did not apply anything to my eyes."

The man from John said, "I do not believe you were ever healed of blindness if He did not put anything on your eyes."

At that moment two denominations came into being. The Mudites and the Anti-Mudites.

It does not matter how you come to know Christ. What does matter is that you know Him. It does not matter whether it happened in an exciting, dramatic way or in a quiet, unobservable manner. It just does not matter how it happened.

Thank God, Scripture does not say you have to be able to identify the precise moment or read a specific chapter or verse, or that it can happen only on a certain day or in a specific way.

Unfortunately, there is a great tendency to look back. What we are called to do is to look forward. As Paul says, *I press toward the mark for the prize of the high calling of God in Christ Jesus* [Phil. 3:14].

Paul says to the Philippians that although he has not grasped everything, he continues to press forward. He says this even though he has not received everything thoroughly. He knew that more would be revealed to him in the future.

He stresses to Christ's followers that he thinks of nothing else, desires nothing else, and knows nothing else, but he continues to press onward. Note, he says this immediately after proclaiming,

> *But what things were gain to me, those I counted loss for Christ.*
> *. . . I count all things but loss for the excellency of the knowledge of Christ Jesus my Lord: . . .*
> *And be found in Him, not having mine own righteousness, . . . but the righteousness which is of God by faith:*
> *That I may know him, and the power of his resurrection, and the fellowship of his sufferings, . . .* [Phil. 3:7–10].

What a statement! That I may know Him more and more, and that my relationship with Him will continue to develop and grow. Paul teaches that we must progress, that the knowledge of Christ is so intricate and difficult that even those who strive after it in this life are not perfect as long as they live.

However, this does not detract from Paul's doctrine or teaching. Why? Because he had received thoroughly that which was sufficient for discharging the office committed to him. Paul responded in faith and actively pursued additional knowledge and prayed for further enlightenment. God blessed him through the Holy Spirit, and God will bless us through the Holy Spirit so that we can perform our responsibilities to Christ according to the hope of our calling.

Paul realized that he was grasped by Christ in order that he might grasp the Lord Jesus. Oh, pray God that we might recognize and accept both of these points since they go hand in hand. *Christ grasps us, so that we might grasp Christ.*

Paul continues by sharing his faith with these words, . . . *but this one thing I do, forgetting those things which are behind, and reaching forth unto those things which are before* [Phil. 3:13].

Paul says that he is *reaching forth* in order to make further progress and is motivated to attain the hope of his calling. He states that his desire is to achieve this one thing and leave everything else behind.

Calvin says the Apostle compares our life *in Christ* with that of the runner and a racecourse. First, it does not profit the runner anything if he begins the race without knowing where the finish line is and continues moving towards it. This applies to us. We have started our walk, and we are to continue pursuing the objective of our calling until death. We are not to cease seeking it until we attain it.

Nowhere does Scripture say we are to *retire* from this race. As a matter of fact, the word "retire," as we define it, does not even appear in Scripture.

It is interesting to note the word "retire" appears only four times in the Old Testament and not once in the New Testament. The meaning in the Old Testament is "to turn, over turn; to cause, to haste; to scatter; or to turn back." But not to "retire" as we think of it today.

As we continue our study of Ephesians, it is revealing to notice the emphasis placed upon pursuing knowledge of the Lord Jesus Christ; receiving the righteousness of God; knowing Him and the power of His Resurrection; being strengthened by His spirit; comprehending *the breadth*, *length*, *depth*, and *height*; and knowing the love of Christ. These things are stressed! Yes, we are to worship God, but there is so much more. There is one thing we are not to do; we are not to retire from this race.

Second, when a runner starts a race he knows that the course is marked out. He realizes if he wanders aimlessly, or allows distractions to get him off course, that he will lose strength and time, and may not finish the race.

God does not want us to wander. He wants us to reach the goal and to be with Him. That is why He provides us with commandments and guidelines.

Third, the runner needs to be unencumbered. He should not allow impediments to deter him, or obstacles to stop him. Therefore, he must not allow his heart and mind to be distracted by irrelevant matters. We are to apply ourselves to God's calling, to the one hope of that calling. Paul does not want us to wander from that high calling. He wants our eyes fixed on the goal.

The Apostle teaches explicitly and forthrightly that he does not think of what has been, but he presses toward the mark. He goes after the prize joyfully, eagerly, and with all the strength he can muster.

Paul condemns looking backward when it destroys, impairs, divides, or distracts. He realizes that anyone who persuades himself that he has made enough progress or has done his duty will become lazy, will abandon the race, and will not apply his mind. He recognized that a person's mind must be turned from these things if he is to earnestly pursue Christ's calling.

It has been mentioned that pursuing these things consists of endeavoring, caring, persevering, knowing, and following the course, all of which are personal and to which we might ascribe personal initiative or industry. However, Paul demolishes these ideas by saying that the reason he presses on for the prize of the high calling of God is Christ Jesus. The pursuit happens because of Christ, not because of me, mine, or myself. Paul declares that this rule applies to each and every member of the community, saying, *Let us therefore . . . be thus minded: and if in anything ye be otherwise minded, God shall reveal even this unto you* [Phil. 3:15].

Each person is to renounce his or her trust in things. The only thing in which we are to glory is Christ's righteousness. We are to prefer His righteousness to everything else. The attaining of righteousness and salvation is possible only in, by, and through Christ Jesus. He, and He alone, makes it possible, not anything in and of ourselves.

The Apostle admonishes the Philippians and tells them not to be proud of their ignorance and not to be obstinate, but to be teachable, to progress by degrees, and to stay on the course. He expresses his complete confidence that God shall reveal His truths and teachings unto them. Paul was fully assured of the reasonableness and truth contained in Christ Jesus and in His teachings.

Calvin points out with clarity what we are to do, why we are to do it, and the benefit of so doing, declaring "that Paul exhorts the Philippians to imitate him, that they may at last reach the same goal, that they may mind the same thing, and walk by the same rule. For where sincere affection flourishes, such as reigned in Paul, the way is easy to a holy and godly concord."

What does Paul mean? Remember, he is addressing the community of believers, not people in general. He wants them to seek God with a pure conscience and to know that the Holy Spirit is working in them, he does not want them to arrogate (assume, seize, claim) anything to themselves, and he wants them to quietly subject their mindset and understanding to Christ. If they will imitate Paul in this matter, then they will experience certain virtues such as pure zeal, fear of the Lord, modesty, and self-renunciation; will accept guidance; will be teachable and loving; and will have a desire for concord and harmony. Paul asks that they imitate him in these things.

He describes the goal of perfection that he wants the members of the community to attain. He presents the doctrine about which they should become knowledgeable and to which they should be in harmony. Then he describes the rule to which they should conform.

We are to look forward, not dwell on what we have been, or where and why. We are not to expend our energies or time on things that may distract or divide. There have been tendencies during the past century and the beginning of this one to focus on things that divide and separate.

Think how groups divide themselves into different age groups, young people, old people, middle-aged people, and other types of groups. We do not find that in the New Testament. An older person may be a babe *in Christ* while a younger person may be spiritually mature. The primary thing is unity *in Christ*.

The New Testament urges us to look forward and to press onward. We may encounter difficulties, obstacles, and problems as we proceed walking with the Lord Jesus. However, we are to look beyond them as we endeavor to overcome them. The Lord Jesus said to His disciples and says to us, *LET not your heart be troubled: ye believe in God, believe also in me* [John 14:1].

Paul tells the Corinthians that Jesus is saying to them: "Do not forget me or ignore me. I am available. Call me, I will listen to you and send the Comforter to be with you." Paul continues, saying,

> *For our light affliction, which is but for a moment, worketh for us*
> *a far more exceeding and eternal weight of glory;*
> *. . . for the things which are seen are temporal; but the things*
> *which are not seen are eternal* [2 Cor. 4:17–18].

The Apostle directs his comments to the Corinthian believers, not to the nonbelievers. This is the special blessing that God grants to members of Christ's body.

What makes, or helps make, the afflictions of this world bearable or seem light? It is transferring our thoughts to the eternal kingdom of God. We are to see the things that are invisible. Paul says to Titus,

> *Teaching us that, denying ungodliness and worldly lusts, we*
> *should live soberly, righteously, and godly, in this present world*
> *(age);*
> *Looking for that blessed hope, and the glorious appearing of the*
> *great God and our Saviour Jesus Christ* [Titus 2:12–13].

The Apostle John says,

> Beloved, now are we the sons (children) of God, and it doth not yet appear what we shall be: but we know that, when he shall appear, we shall be like him; for we shall see him as he is [1 John 3:2].

These truths were written to the community of believers.

Unfortunately, we constantly look at the present instead of the future. This is only natural since for the most part man lives in the present. He or she is concerned with current developments and fads, not with things eternal.

However, in the things of the Spirit, and with the community of believers, we are to look to the future. *For now we see through a glass* (mirror), *darkly* (dimly); *but then face to face: now I know in part; but then shall I know even as also I am known* [1 Cor. 13:12].

Remember, we shall not only see Him, we shall be like Him. Therefore, should we not want to look forward? Should we not be joyful about being *called in one hope of your calling* [Eph. 4:4]? May God grant us the ability to look forward, to walk in fellowship with the Lord Jesus Christ, and *to be strengthened with might by his Spirit in the inner man* [Eph. 3:16].

> IF ye then be risen with Christ, seek those things which are above, where Christ sitteth on the right hand of God.
> Set your affection (mind) on things above, not on things on the earth [Col. 3:1–2].

Please note, the Apostle says, *set your affection* (mind) *on things above*. What does he mean? Not what you would normally think. The Greek word used is *phroneō* which means "to mind" or "to think." Therefore, set your mind, your thinking on Christ until the day you cross over the bar. You are not to retire in this world.

Amen!

9

King of Kings, Lord of Lords

One Lord, one faith, one baptism, . . . [Eph. 4:5].

The community of believers is the work of the Holy Trinity. During the past four chapters we have focused upon and considered the Holy Spirit. Now, we turn our attention to the Son, the blessed Lord Jesus Christ.

The word *Lord* appears innumerable times in both the Old and New Testaments. However, during the period just before the birth of Christ and in the first century, the terms gods and lords were used interchangeably and had much the same meaning to the pagans of this period as well.

But to the early members of the community of believers there was only *one God* and *one Lord*: The *one God* is the Father and the *one Lord* is Jesus Christ.

The early followers called God by the term *Lord* whether they were quoting from the Old Testament or not. However, in the New Testament Epistles Paul boldly applies to the Lord Jesus Christ certain Old Testament passages in which the term *Lord* meant God or God Almighty.

It is stated by many scholars that when Paul used the term *Lord* he always meant the "Lord Jesus Christ." Further, "except in Old Testament quotations it is doubtful whether in his letters 'the Lord' ever means anything but the Lord Jesus Christ," as appropriately noted by J.V. Campbell.

When examining this verse, it is well to consider what the early members of the community called Jesus. The early Gentile followers called Him *Lord,* and so did His disciples. The early Jews who were converted and baptized, and accepted Christ, and those who were raised in the strict monotheism of the Old Testament called Him *Lord*.

What about this title *Lord,* or as it is in the Greek, *Kyrios*? It surpasses the designations of Messiah or Son of Man and is the highest title bestowed upon Him. Jesus also used the term in referring to Himself.

> *Not every one that saith unto me, Lord, Lord, shall enter into the kingdom of heaven; but he that doeth the will of my Father which is in heaven* [Matt. 7:21].

> *Ye call me Master* (Teacher) *and Lord: and ye say well; for so I am* [John 13:13].

Paul calls Jesus *Lord* or *Our Lord* but maintains Jesus' subordination to God the Father, saying, *. . . every tongue should confess that Jesus Christ is Lord, to the glory of God the Father* [Phil. 2:11].

The important point is not when the title *Kyrios* first came into use, but the way it is used to describe Jesus. What is revealed in the New Testament, especially in Paul's letters, concerning the term *Kyrios*?

Paul calls on the Lord Jesus Christ as well as God the Father in prayer. He prayed to Jesus without naming the Father and received an answer when the Lord said unto him, *My grace is sufficient unto thee: for my strength* (power) *is made perfect in weakness* [2 Cor. 12:9].

When considering these things, it is well to remember Paul's birth, training, and zeal. Undoubtedly, he did not think there was any blasphemy in praying as he did and identifying Jesus as *Kyrios,* or *Lord.* Probably, the most notable expression by Paul on this matter is in writing to the Philippians,

> *Wherefore God also hath highly exalted him, and given him a name which is above every name:*
> *That at the name of Jesus every knee should bow, of things* (those) *in heaven, and things* (those) *in earth, and things* (those) *under the earth;*
> *And that every tongue should confess that Jesus Christ is Lord, to the glory of God the Father* [Phil. 2:9–11].

In the New Testament the name of God is ascribed to Jesus. It is that name which is the epitome of God's self-expression.

It should be noted that "whoever speaks of Kyrios is speaking of God, of God as revealed in His Lordship, or in His Son. The question of Christ's deity and its implications are to be considered in the New Testament framework; primarily in connection with His work rather than His being," as Otto Weber amplifies upon the truths contained in Scripture for our edification.

Second, we are to consider the Lord Jesus Christ as our Master yesterday, today, and tomorrow. The term *Kyrios* means the present Lord, not someone who lived in the past, and that person is Jesus, our Lord.

The proper behavior in our relationship to *Kyrios* is serving and obeying Him. Paul describes the proper behavior in his letter to the Romans, saying,

> *Be kindly affectioned* (affectionate) *one to another with brotherly love; in honor preferring* (in giving preference to) *one another;*
> *Not slothful* (lagging in diligence) *in business; fervent in spirit; serving the Lord;*
> *Rejoicing in hope; patient* (persevering) *in tribulation; continuing* (steadfastly) *instant in prayer;*
> *Distributing to the necessity* (needs) *of saints; given to hospitality* [Rom. 12:10–13].

These are not onerous commands, they are uplifting. They produce joy and strength for walking with Jesus. Consider each of these commands and embrace them one by one as you continue your walk with Jesus.

These ten commands are not always easy to do. They require discipline and effort, which the members of Christ's body are to exhibit. Paul adds additional impact to these commands by saying,

> *And whatsoever ye do, do it heartily, as to the Lord, and not unto men;*
> *Knowing that of the Lord ye shall receive the reward of the inheritance: for ye serve the Lord Christ.*
> *But he that doeth wrong shall receive for the wrong which he hath done: and there is no respect of persons* [Col. 3:23–25].

These words are tough meat. They tell what is required to serve the Lord Christ. They also tell us what will happen if we do not obey Him. In addition, Paul reinforces these truths with the admonition:

> *That ye might walk worthy of the Lord unto all pleasing, being fruitful in every good work, and increasing in the knowledge of God* [Col. 1:10].

Again, Paul commands us to increase in knowledge. It also confirms that the Lord is the living and commanding authority.

Paul's writings amplify upon and support Christ, saying,

> *Not every one that saith unto me, Lord, Lord, shall enter into the kingdom of heaven; but he that doeth the will of my Father which is in heaven* [Matt. 7:21].

When considering these verses, hopefully you see God in Christ; Christ as the *Lord, Kyrios*; the community of believers receiving its being and total existence from Christ; the community being under His command and subject to His final judgment; and that He is the Master.

Third, *Kyrios* denotes the one who is *Lord* of the world. He is not only Master of the community; He is *Lord* of the entire world.

> *Being confident of this very thing, that he which hath begun a good work in you will perform* (complete) *it until the day of Jesus Christ* [Phil. 1:6].

> *Henceforth there is laid up for me a crown of righteousness, which the Lord, the righteous judge, shall give me at that day: and not to me only, but unto all them also that love his appearing* [2 Tim. 4:8].

Jesus' supreme authority is seen in Scripture where He is called *King of Kings, Lord of Lords*. The New Testament speaks not only of God's kingly rule, but also of Jesus' kingly rule. Paul says to the Ephesians,

> *For this ye know, that no whoremonger, nor unclean person, nor covetous man, who is an idolater, hath any inheritance in the kingdom of Christ and of God* [Eph. 5:5].

> *Then said Jesus unto his disciples, . . .* [Matt. 16:24].

> *Verily I say unto you, There be some standing here, which shall not taste of death, till they see the Son of man coming in his kingdom* [Matt. 16:28].

Fourth, He is the Son of God. Jesus has the title *Kyrios* and also is known as the Son of God. The *Kyrios* title differs from the Son of God title as follows: it is directed to the presence of Jesus and to His legitimacy, but it does not merge with statements about the Father. In expressing the distinctiveness of Jesus from the Father and His subordination to the Father, it notes that Jesus is from the Father, He is not out of Himself, nor is He out of the world. Further, God the Father certifies Jesus as His Son and knows Him as the Son from heaven, saying, *And there came a voice from heaven, saying, Thou art my beloved Son, in whom I am well pleased* [Mark 1:11].

The Father also has delivered all things unto the Son. Jesus affirms this, saying,

> *All things are delivered unto me of my Father: and no man knoweth the Son, but the Father; neither knoweth any man the*

> *Father, save* (except) *the Son, and he to whomsoever the Son will reveal him* [Matt. 11:27].

In addition, the title Son of God contains additional thoughts and concepts, notably that Jesus is the servant of God and also in God's eternity. This is seen in the pre-existence of Jesus; the One who has come out of God's eternity, not just out of time; the only begotten Son of God; and God's resounding statement, *This is my beloved Son.*

Fifth, the title *Kyrios* is applied to Jesus' deity. The New Testament witness to Christ is not only seen in the few passages which speak of Him as God, but also in the context of the New Testament and presenting Him to the community of believers.

This deity is seen in the title of *Majesty*, subordination to the will of the Father, and *my beloved Son*. It is also seen clearly in Philippians through Paul's majestic, revealing statement,

> *Let this mind be in you, which was also in Christ Jesus:*
> *Who, being in the form of God, thought it not robbery to be equal with God:*
> *... took upon him the form of a servant, ...*
> *... humbled himself, and became obedient unto death, even the death of the cross.*
> *Wherefore God also hath highly exalted him, ...*
> *That at the name of Jesus every knee should bow, ...*
> *And that every tongue should confess that Jesus Christ is Lord, to the glory of God the Father* [Phil. 2:5–11].

Jesus' being, actions, and words, though equal with God are to be grasped as emanating from the One who is the Son of God. He *humbled himself*, took the *form of a servant*, and was *obedient unto death*.

Although Jesus possessed a certain honor and position, He did what He did. He acted "in sovereign divine freedom," as appropriately described by an unknown author. Consider the contents of these verses,

> *But to us there is but one God, the Father, of whom are all things, and we in* (for) *him; and one Lord Jesus Christ, by whom are all things, and we* (live) *by him* [1 Cor. 8:6].

> *For in Him dwelleth all the fullness of the Godhead bodily* [Col. 2:9].

> *Looking for that blessed hope, and the glorious appearing of the great God and our Saviour Jesus Christ* [Titus 2:13].

These statements refer to Jesus' deity and to the work of God the Father in Him.

We have previously considered the person of the Holy Spirit. Now we are focusing our attention on the Lord Jesus Christ. This is only natural because . . . *no man can say that Jesus is Lord, but by the Holy Ghost* [1 Cor. 12:3]. It is the Holy Ghost who leads us to the Lord Jesus and allows us to see Him and to know Him.

Another reason Paul proceeds to speak of the Son is that he has already presented the *one body* which is the community of believers. Therefore, he must present the head, because a body cannot function without a head. The Apostle also feels called upon to emphasize the unity of the church or community. He does this with the two words, *One Lord*. He states it as simply and emphatically as possible. It is the one Lord Jesus Christ who not only leads to unity but produces it. Probably the best approach to understanding the biblical Doctrine of Unity is to focus on the Lord Jesus. Paul says, *Endeavoring to keep the unity of the Spirit in the bond of peace* [Eph. 4:3].

There are two important questions to consider. What are the implications? How are we to interpret the Apostle's emphasis upon the *One Lord*? Of primary importance is the truth that Christ, and Christ alone, is Christianity. Conversely, Christianity is Christ. It is not a collection of ideas or thoughts, or a philosophy or a teaching. All these things may vary, and they tend to divide.

There is only *One Lord* and there should be unity with Him. The real danger threatening the community of believers is forgetting or ignoring the Lord Jesus. We should not allow anything to come between us and the Lord. We are to know Him, acquire knowledge of Him, and remain close to Him.

There is a second important point. There is only *One Lord* and He cannot be divided. Paul tells the Corinthians that they are trying to divide Christ, and that this cannot be done. Christ is One, and He is indivisible.

This leads to the doctrine of the two natures in one person. The two natures are so joined together that they cannot be separated—Christ as God and Christ as man. Possibly it is better stated as God in man or in the form of man. It is not a case of Christ as God or Christ as man and the one is separate from the other. That is not to be done. Christ is always God-man.

There is only one Christ. There are not many christs. When I believe in Him I am in the same position as all the others who believe in Him. There is *One Lord* and one community.

We are to accept and emphasize that the *Lord* is unique in His work. The New Testament stresses the fact that there is one and only one Saviour. To deny this is to deny the most essential truth of the New Testament and the Christian faith.

"Another point to stress regarding faith in Christ is its intolerance. Yes, there is an intolerant aspect regarding faith in Christ. Many statements in Scripture assert that to place anyone on the same level as Christ or to discuss salvation apart from Him is a denial of the truth.

"At one and the same time Christianity is intolerant and unifying—'Though we or an angel from heaven preach any other gospel to you than that which we have preached unto you, let him be accursed;' says Paul (Gal. 1:8). If an angel from heaven, he says, comes and preaches to you and he denies what I have told you about this blessed person, let him be accursed. He was intolerant and we must be intolerant. We must not put anyone near Him, He is alone; and we must never say that God can be known without Him. We must be utterly intolerant at this point. And because all true Christians are intolerant at this point, and all are in Him, they are all united, welded into one. Intolerance, and absolute unity. Is not this the New Testament Gospel? We must preserve both. We must say at one and the same time, that there cannot be such a thing as a World Congress of Faiths and also that all true Christians are one in Christ Jesus. It is precisely because we are all one in Christ that you cannot have a World Congress of Faiths. Such an idea is a farce; indeed, it is a denial of Christ. Christianity cannot participate in such a Congress. It cannot enter into any proposal or conference that says that Christianity is marvelous, but, after all, God gave insights to the Buddha, to Confucius, Mahomet and others and we can learn from them. The Christian does not need to learn from such quarters, because 'all the treasures of wisdom and knowledge are in Christ'. He does not need them, is not interested in them, because he has it all in Himself. Even to give a glance at any other is a denial of Him. Intolerant, and yet unifying!" as expressed by Martyn Lloyd-Jones in accord with the truths contained in the New Testament.

What did Peter say when he addressed the Sanhedrin? *Neither is there salvation in any other: for there is none other name under heaven given among men, whereby we must be saved* [Acts 4:12].

The authorities were trying to prohibit Peter and the other apostles from preaching and working miracles in the name of Christ. Peter said there is no other name. There is not a second, third, or fourth name. It is Christ and Christ alone. There is none other who is God and man, who is God in man. He did it all. He left nothing undone.

The Corinthians were not clear about this point. Though they believed in the one God, they thought there were other gods and lords. Paul addresses this point, saying to them,

> *For though there be that are called gods, whether in heaven or in earth, (as there be gods many, and lords many,)*
> *But to us there is but one God, the Father, of whom are all things, and we in* (for) *him; and one Lord Jesus Christ, by whom are all things, and we* (live) *by him* [1 Cor. 8:5–6].

There is only *one God* and *one Lord Jesus Christ*. There is only One who can come between God and an individual, and that is the Lord Jesus Christ. Consider the following questions:

- How do we pray to God?
- How do we go to God?
- How do we listen to God?
- How do we have access to God?

The answer to these and all similar questions is the same, by the Lord Jesus Christ.

There is only one mediator, and only one Saviour. There will never be another, because there is no need for another. He has done it all. The incarnation is unique. The crucifixion is unique. The resurrection is unique. The Lord Jesus Christ is unique. He is the unique Son of God.

What does all this mean? If we are to have a full and clear perception of God and Christ, if we are to have assurance of understanding in faith, if we are not to vacillate and waver, then we must have a knowledge of the Gospel.

God cannot be known other than through Christ, and the Father is known where Christ is known. The Apostle John wrote,

> *Whosoever denieth the Son, the same hath not the Father;* (but) *he that acknowledgeth the Son hath the Father also* [1 John 2:23].

> *He that hath the Son hath* (the) *life; and he that hath not the Son of God hath not* (the) *life* [1 John 5:12].

A person is ignorant of Christ who is not led by Him to the Father and who does not fully embrace God in Him. This reveals the deity of Christ and the essence of His unity with the Father.

Paul says, *In whom are hid all the treasures of wisdom and knowledge* [Col. 2:3]. What does he mean? All the treasures of wisdom and knowledge are hidden in Christ. If we truly know Christ, then we can have God's wisdom through Him. God reveals Himself through the Son, and it is all included in the Gospel.

These treasures are hidden "in the contemptible humility and simplicity of the cross. It is here that we obtain knowledge, wisdom, learning and understanding. Not anywhere else," according to the wisdom and humility of John Calvin.

Jesus Christ is our Lord and Master. He is the *One Lord* and the one Master. Jesus said to His disciples on the night He was betrayed,

> *Ye call me Master* (Teacher) *and Lord: and ye say well for so I am.*
> *If I then, your Lord and Master* (Teacher), *have washed your feet; ye also ought to wash one another's feet* [John 13:13–14].

Jesus is saying, whoever you are, I am the Master and ye are the servants, and if I have done something, then you are to do it. He is emphasizing the will of God, obedience, knowledge, prayer, and self-denial. *HE THAT GLORIETH, LET HIM GLORY IN THE LORD* [2 Cor. 10:17]. May we mature in the faith to the point where we echo the words of Paul in truth and humility.

Ephesians makes it more and more evident that the central figure in this wonderful Epistle is not the Jesus of history, but the living Lord Jesus Christ. We are redeemed through His love; we are brought into His presence. He is the *one Lord*. He is Himself. He is Lord of Lords, the Lord God almighty. He is the Head of the community of believers, His Headship is mediated by the Holy Spirit, and He is what we confess Him to be, *My Lord and My God.*

Amen!

10

Thy Blood Shed for Me

> One Lord, one faith, one baptism, . . . [Eph. 4:5].

Our attention now focuses upon the two words *one faith* as stated in *One Lord, one faith, one baptism* [Eph. 4:5].

The Apostle Paul is truly amazing in the way he presents the Gospel of Jesus Christ, in how he communicates the great truths and teachings, in how he ties things together, and in how he places emphasis on certain points.

Please note how Paul stresses unity in the first sixteen verses of the fourth chapter,

- *Endeavoring to keep the unity of the Spirit . . .* [Eph. 4:3];
- using the word *one* seven times in verses four, five, and six;
- *Till we all come in* (into) *the unity of the faith, and of the knowledge of the Son of God, unto a perfect* (mature) *man, unto the measure of the stature of the fullness of Christ* [Eph. 4:13]; and
- then describing the benefits bestowed upon the members of the community in verses fourteen, fifteen, and sixteen.

Consider the term *one faith*. Paul places this term immediately after *One Lord*. He does not place it with the grouping on the Holy Spirit or with the Father in the next verse. Why?

Many learned commentators seem troubled by this phrase. There is disagreement as to its exact meaning. Basically, there are two points of view.

Some believe the term refers to our subjective faith and that inward quality or capacity enabling us to believe. They maintain that the character or nature of faith is patently the same in all believers. They all have the same actions, same awareness of mind, and same feelings. Further, that everything about the faith of a believer is subjectively the same.

What about this line of reasoning? The Apostle is endeavoring to provide absolute proof for a believer's faith that when he is assailed by doubts and temptations, God's truths will sustain him. Whenever you want to demonstrate, or prove, something you should not resort to the subjective or personal. Subjective reasoning does not provide much strength against objective attacks. The Apostle, in these verses, is providing objective proof, not subjective reasons. Therefore, *one faith* should not be considered subjectively.

On the other hand, there are those who argue that *one faith* is strictly objective and refers to an objective body of truth that is believed. Further, that it is the individual's act of believing. This point of view raises another difficulty. Those who hold to this tend to say that Paul is referring to a complete compendium, or confession of faith. For example, they argue that all those professing belief *in Christ* should adopt and subscribe to one of the great Confessions of Faith such as the Westminster Confession of Faith, the Heidelberg Confession, or the 39 Articles of the Church of England. They say that *one faith* means "a complete outline and description of what we believe," to quote and paraphrase the renowned Martyn Lloyd-Jones.

That is not a satisfactory explanation. It generates differences of opinion and divisions, which do not lead to Paul's statement, *Till we all come in the unity of the faith, and of the knowledge of the Son of God* [Eph. 4:13].

The Apostle appears to be saying that although we may not agree on everything, there is a day coming when we will be brought together in unity. Therefore, it seems clear that we cannot take this expression to mean complete agreement about every detail in a theological commentary.

How is the Apostle using the term *one faith*? It appears he is using it as a thesis or persuasion for unity. It is as definite as one Lord, one Spirit, and one God. *One faith* is something about which all members of the community must be in agreement.

What does it mean? Faith in the New Testament is the revealed, divine truth essential for salvation, delivered unto the saints once and for all. It is the very foundation of unity in the body of Christ. Ruth Paxson states it beautifully, effectively, and pointedly, saying, "Faith is the way of access unto God through an act of believing in the Lord Jesus Christ, who is the heart of the faith."

The faith gives us a Person in whom to believe. Faith accepts the gift and receives the Person. The faith of the community of believers, or the Christian faith, is essentially faith in Christ.

This may be generally accepted, but what does it mean? First, it means that it is faith in Christ. It is an attitude and a relationship to the Person of Jesus Christ. It is not directed toward objective issues. It is directed toward the Person, and the issues are secondary.

This faith is obedience, trust, and self-surrender to a person, not to issues or other facts. This faith in Jesus Christ is never directly oriented toward propositions, however true they may be, or to certain points of view, even if they may be correct. This faith goes first to Jesus Christ, and then it goes to other things, other propositions, viewpoints, or issues. This faith is faith in Jesus Christ, and by it we encounter God's own truth, which conquers us, and by it God Himself is revealed to us in His Word and by His Spirit.

Second, in this faith a person encounters and deals with Jesus Christ, the Person. We must realize that each of us is a person as we do this. It is an act committed by a person. Some may say that it is a decision by a person. This can be misunderstood and misinterpreted.

Faith is not submission when confronted by certain facts or accepting stronger arguments. In a sense, it is not merely the act of the intellect or will, but of the whole person.

This faith brings me to the Person of Jesus Christ just as I am, as myself, without my defenses or my ego. It reveals me unprotected and insecure. I cannot surround myself with my past, my desires, my professions, my intentions, my relationships, my comparisons, or anything else of mine. My faith is not based upon this world, but it redirects every part of my being toward this world, the people, and things surrounding me.

Third, faith is temporal. This statement may raise an eyebrow or two. Faith deals with the here and now. It does not deal with something timeless or in the future. It does not lift us out of our present time but radically Jesus Christ meets us in history, in the history of His community, and in our history. This faith, believing in Jesus Christ, happens in time, which is God's time, and it happens without our being able to speculate about it after the fact.

We have examined faith and considered applicable descriptions. Let us return to an earlier question. What does Paul mean by the term *one faith*? After devoting time to the material presented consider the following: The New Testament frequently deals with a specific and great message concerning salvation, "Justification by Faith." The Apostle, in this portion of Ephesians, is dealing with the very essence of the Gospel, one Spirit, one Lord, one faith, and one Father. Possibly the Apostle is referring to a justifying faith, and in his description it is not only the *one faith*, it is the only faith.

The renowned John Calvin states, "If we seek salvation, i.e. life with God, we must first seek righteousness, by which we may be reconciled to Him, and obtain that life which consists in His benevolence alone through His being favorable to us."

The word of faith in the eighth verse is the word of justification by faith. It is the word about faith as the justifying principle in the sense that the just shall live by faith. One Lord, one faith, one baptism. The one faith is the only faith. Paul amplifies upon this in his letter to the Romans saying,"

> *For I am not ashamed of the gospel of Christ: for it is the power of God unto salvation to every one that believeth; to the Jew first, and also to the Greek.*
>
> *For therein is the righteousness of God revealed from faith to faith: as it is written, THE JUST SHALL LIVE BY FAITH* [Rom. 1:16–17].
>
> *Therefore by the deeds of the law there shall no flesh be justified in his sight: for by the law is the knowledge of sin.*
>
> *But now the righteousness of God without* (apart from) *the law is manifested, being witnessed by the law and the prophets;*
>
> *Even the righteousness of God which is by faith of Jesus Christ unto all and upon all them that believe: for there is no difference:*
>
> *For all have sinned, and come* (fall) *short of the glory of God* [Rom. 3:20–23].
>
> *But what saith it? THE WORD IS NIGH (NEAR) THEE, EVEN IN THY MOUTH, AND IN THY HEART: that is, the word of faith, which we preach;*
>
> *That if thou shalt confess with thy mouth the Lord Jesus, and shalt believe in thine heart that God hath raised him from the dead, thou shalt be saved* [Rom. 10:8–9].

The one faith was rediscovered or, if you will, revealed once again, and restored during the Reformation. It was preached by the Reformation fathers. It was rediscovered in the great principle, *The just shall live by faith* [Rom. 1:17]. It is not faith in general, but it is a specific message about the way of justification, which is by the *one faith*.

We are not dealing with subjective feelings about faith, nor a compendium, nor a confession of faith. The message concerning God's way is righteousness, which is from God. It is not something people do. It is what God has done and is doing. It is God who justifies the ungodly. It is God's way. It is God's act!

The Apostle states this in various ways. *But to him that worketh not, but believeth on him that justifieth the ungodly, his faith is counted for* (imputed as) *righteousness* [Rom. 4:5]. God makes us acceptable in His sight. God makes it possible for us to be right with Him and for us to be reconciled to Him. God does this, and He does it in Christ Jesus. God proclaims that we are righteous. It is God's action that justifies us. God pronounces that we are just and free from sin.

How does God do this? How can God justify the ungodly? Paul answers these questions saying simply, yet profoundly, that we are . . . *justified freely* (without any cost) *by his grace through the redemption that is in Christ Jesus* [Rom. 3:24].

God takes our sins and puts them on Christ, and punishes them in that way. This is the faith we are to grasp and to believe—that God was in Christ reconciling the world unto Himself.

He does not impute their trespasses unto them. He has done this that we might be made the righteousness of God in Him.

The heart of this message is that God has taken our sins and imputed them to Christ. He has placed them on Christ's account, not ours. He has punished them in Christ, and as the Gospel says, *For he hath made him to be sin for us, who knew no sin* [2 Cor. 5:21].

God has gone even further. He has placed Christ's righteousness on our account. The Lord Jesus never sinned, He obeyed the law in every detail, yet the Father placed His righteousness on our account. Our unrighteousness was placed on Him. His righteousness was placed on us. What a deal! How can we ignore it or refuse it?

The *word faith* is that our salvation is God's act, completely and fully, through the Lord Jesus Christ. That is why the phrase *one faith* follows *One Lord*. The *One Lord* was sent by the *one Father*. We contribute nothing. Our deeds, our actions, our words mean nothing. It is all from God. It is all God's grace. It is God's doing from Alpha to Omega.

God's righteousness is placed upon us. It is the righteousness of Christ. All of our righteousness is *in Christ*, and it is there by faith and faith alone. The righteousness of Christ is given to us and becomes ours through faith, which is also the gift of God.

How long has God been bestowing the gift of Christ's righteousness and His faith? Since the time of Abraham.

Paul states *one faith* at this particular time. Why? Because he is concerned about unity, and he wants us to see this unity. Paul points out specifically and positively that righteousness and faith always have been the only way of salvation. Paul amplifies upon this with his words of wisdom to the Romans, saying,

> . . . for we say that faith was reckoned (imputed) to Abraham for righteousness.
> *How was it then reckoned? when he was in circumcision, or in uncircumcision? . . .*
> *And he received the sign of circumcision, a seal of the righteousness of the faith which he had yet being uncircumcised: that he might be the father of all them that believe, though they be not circumcised; . . .*
> *And the father of circumcision to them who are not of the circumcision only, but who also walk in the steps of that faith of our father Abraham, which he had being yet uncircumcised* [Rom. 4:9–12].

Abraham is the father of us all. The father of all who believe the faith, in the one faith.

The eleventh chapter of Hebrews teaches us that faith goes back further than Abraham. The author describes the faith of Abel, Enoch, and Noah, who lived long before Abraham. Further, he says, *But without faith it is impossible to please him* (God): *for he that cometh to God must believe that he is, and that he is a rewarder of them that diligently seek him* [Heb. 11:6]. God has always justified men by faith. There was not one way to be justified in the Old Testament and another in the New Testament. The people in the Old Testament were justified by faith. It is *one faith*; it has always been *one faith*.

There is only one way of salvation. It is the gift of faith whereby the righteousness of Christ is imputed to us after our sins have been imputed to Him. As John Calvin states unequivocally, "Those who are righteousness by faith are righteous outside themselves, that is in Christ."

Those people who renounce any confidence in works and rely fully and completely on the promise of God are of the *one faith*. And to be of that *one faith* means placing one's righteousness and hope of salvation in God's mercy. If Abraham was justified by faith, then we his children must stand firmly in the faith. The members of the community are the children of Abraham; if they are not the children of Abraham, then they are not members of the community.

Paul prefaced his statements in Ephesians 4:4–6 by saying, *Endeavoring to keep the unity of the Spirit in the bond of peace* [Eph. 4:3]. We are to have and to keep this unity in the *one faith*. We have seen how we can receive this unity.

Therefore, a question: how can we break this unity with respect to the *one faith*? There are several ways. One is by bringing in something of our own, such as our "good" life, or our "good" works, boasting about our good deeds, our piety, our lives, our achievements, our contributions, our prayers, and anything else that we claim as ours. Any one of these things is a denial of the principle of faith.

A second way is by denying the absolute centrality of Christ and His work. People say they are saved and their sins are forgiven. However, they never mention the Lord Jesus Christ.

They say God is a God of love, and since He is, He forgives everyone and would not let anyone go to hell. These people attribute everything to God. They think and act as though Jesus had never lived, had never gone to the Cross, and had never shed His blood. They ignore the Lord Jesus Christ. They believe that either forgiveness is automatic, or that it is received apart from Jesus Christ.

A third way to break unity is by adding requirements to this *one faith*. Some say that unity can be realized by faith plus circumcision; how the sacraments are transmitted; how they are baptized; certain saints; and adding anything, and that means anything, to the *one faith*.

There is only one thing essential to salvation or a right relationship with God and that is *One Lord, one faith*. That *one faith* is a justifying faith, just as it was for Abraham, David, and the rest.

There is only *one faith* and one way of salvation. It is stated very simply, forthrightly, and truthfully in two hymns of old, Rock of Ages,

Cleft for Me by Augustus Toplady and Just as I am, Without Plea by Charlotte Elliott,

> *Nothing in my hand I bring,*
> *simply to thy cross I cling;*
> *Naked, come to Thee for dress,*
> *Helpless look to Thee for grace;*
> *Foul, to the fountain fly;*
> *Wash me, Saviour, or I die.*
>
> *While I draw this fleeting breath,*
> *When my eyelids close in death,*
> *When I soar to worlds unknown,*
> *See Thee on Thy judgment throne,"*
> *Rock of Ages, cleft for me,*
> *Let me hide myself in Thee. Amen.*

and

> *Just as I am without one plea*
> *But that thy blood was shed for me,*
> *And thou bidst me come to Thee,*
> *O Lamb of God, I come, I come.*

One Lord, one faith. Thank God it is a justifying faith. Amen!

11

Baptism

One Lord, one faith, one baptism, . . . [Eph. 4:5].

Now it is time to focus attention on the last two words of this meaningful verse, *One lord, one faith, one baptism, . . .*

What is meant by the term *baptism*? Webster defines it as "a Christian sacrament signifying spiritual rebirth and admitting the recipient to the Christian community through the ritual use of water," and also as "a rite using water for spiritual purification" or "an act, experience by which one is purified, sanctified, initiated or named."

Of course, there may be other definitions. However, two questions are of primary importance when considering this term:

- What does Scripture say about baptism?
- What does Paul mean when he uses the term?

Baptism always comes first when members of the community make proclamations about their activities and state the requirements for membership. It signifies visible membership into the community of believers.

Entry into the community of believers is not a legal act which a person freely makes, nor is it the result of his or her faith. Nor is it constituted by one's birth.

There are several essential ingredients for baptism. First, it establishes membership in the community of believers, whether an infant, child, or adult. It occurs through a physical event and requires water.

The words *baptize* and *baptism* go back to the Greek word *bapto* which means "to dip." Also, it means "to wash" and as we interpret it, "to wash oneself." In the Old Testament there is the word *baptizein*, which also means "to dip." In the New Testament the Greek words used are:

- *Baptisma*, which means "as a state" and is used in the verse we are examining; and
- *Baptize*, which means "to consecrate by pouring out on, or putting into."

Also, it may mean "to baptize."

Baptism is a physical act. This means there is action. It is not a passive event. We become members of the community of believers by a physical act, not as a result of baptismal doctrine.

Second, the baptismal event always involves the actions of another person. It is not an individual act. Individuals are involved, but it takes at least two people to perform the act.

There is no available evidence of anyone baptizing himself, not even the Lord Jesus. We are brought to the baptismal font, whether we are a babe, an aged adult, or in between. And it is the minister or priest who performs the baptismal rite.

It should be noted that the person being baptized accepts the act passively whether as an infant, child, or adult. This is important.

The person baptized becomes a member of the community of believers. He or she does not make themselves members of the community. They are made members of it.

Third, the act of baptism does not take place between an individual and a church fellowship. It takes place through the process of being incorporated into the body of Christ. The community into which the baptized person becomes a member is the body of Christ.

Fourth, baptism is not a silent event. When it takes place the Word is proclaimed, and God's promise is spoken. It happens in the name of the Father, Son, and Holy Spirit. The important ingredient in the baptismal event is the name, the name that is proclaimed. And that name is the Lord Jesus Christ. Baptism cannot take place without that name, the promise cannot be received without it, and a claim cannot be made without proclaiming that name.

During the first sixteen verses of the fourth chapter, Paul stresses unity. His teachings and the application of doctrine in the first three chapters are directed toward unity.

We all know and recognize that the act of baptism has created divisions. Yet the Apostle emphasizes unity. What points should be considered? First, consider some negatives. Throughout the centuries people have taught that *one baptism* refers to baptismal regeneration. In other words, they teach that baptism is the means of regeneration. Therefore, anyone who is baptized receives a new life and is regenerated. They say the infant or child is now regenerated. They believe there is regeneration solely and only through the instrumentality of baptism, that it is the act of baptism that regenerates a person.

Second, some express baptism only by the mode of administering it. However, this cannot be the explanation since the *one baptism* is presented within the context of unity. The idea of performing the sacrament of baptism in only one way leads to division.

A third interpretation is that *one baptism* refers only to the rite of baptism. They believe that the Apostle was only stating the idea that when people become Christians they are baptized, and further, that the baptismal event was their initiation into the visible community.

We need to beware of making baptism essential to salvation. Further, baptismal regeneration is not taught in Scripture. It was introduced in order to strengthen the power of the priesthood and the church. We cannot say, we must not say, that baptism is essential to salvation or that a person cannot be saved unless he or she is baptized. Remember the thief on the Cross.

What is the basis for baptism? How was it effectively established? How can we grasp its essence? These questions must be addressed. There is nothing in the baptismal event that conveys an understanding of it. It is a concrete, physical act in which the Word and the Lord Jesus Christ are both proclaimed and claimed. Where is the validity of baptism? How is this act valid before God, derived from God, and connected to God?

First, the connecting factor is the Holy Spirit and the knowledge of faith, which confirms itself in baptism. It can be the faith of the community, or of the person performing the act, or the person being baptized. Faith comes first. Remember Philip and the eunuch, and Lydia, *whose heart the Lord opened* [Acts 16:14], and Paul and the jailer, and *One Lord, one faith, one baptism* [Eph. 4:5]. The New Testament does not say that baptism is based upon faith, or that it is essential to confirming faith.

There is an interesting fact here. We have faith only as we receive it. And we have baptism only as we receive it. Faith and baptism belong together. Baptism does not result from faith, and faith does not result from baptism.

Second, baptism allows us to share in the death and resurrection of the Lord Jesus Christ. In Romans, Paul describes one impact of being baptized. The person is submersed into the death of Christ and then receives newness of life. When considering this, remember that baptism is an act of separation, of setting aside, and it results in being integrated into the community of believers and into a new reality.

Baptism provides for participating in the body of Christ. The baptized person is *in Christ* and is a "new creation."

Remember, in both faith and baptism man is the receiver. He receives that which Jesus Christ has done for him.

A serious question: how do I receive through the act of baptism the personal work of the Lord Jesus Christ? Paul addresses this question and appropriately provides the following explanation: *For if we have been planted* (united) *together in the likeness of his death,* (certainly) *we shall be also in the likeness of his resurrection* [Rom. 6:5].

Baptism is a sign. However, it is not a bare and empty sign. It is a sign of great force and efficacy. It is a means of grace. The grace it signifies is presented and applied to us.

The promises expressed at the time of baptism are assured and accomplished for all those who are baptized, if they believe them and claim them.

Third, the basis and power of baptism is the living and present Lord Jesus Christ. *One Lord, one faith, one baptism* [Eph. 4:5]. Baptism has its basis in Jesus Christ, the same person who is the mediator and guarantor of the new covenant.

The community of believers is the place, organ, and witness to the new covenant. Baptism is the means by which we affirm God's grace, or claim that grace for ourselves and our children. It is through this sacrament that an individual may become a member of the community of believers. The community lives as an assembly. It lives for one Lord, by one faith, through one baptism.

When we are *in Christ*, God says yes to a man, or to the community. It is in the name of Jesus Christ that the community says yes to God.

What does *one baptism* represent and signify?

- The first thing to emphasize is that baptism is into one name only, the Lord Jesus Christ.

- The baptism "into Christ" is baptism into union with Him, into possession by Him, into all the benefits He bestows on us, such as justification and sanctification.
- Baptism into the Lord Jesus Christ means unity, not division.

Paul asks, *Is Christ divided? was Paul crucified for you? or were ye baptized in the name of Paul* [1 Cor. 1:13]? Of course not! They were all baptized in the name of the Lord Jesus Christ. One Lord, one justifying faith, one baptism in the name of the Lord Jesus Christ.

Being baptized in the name of the Lord Jesus Christ is emphasized in the Acts of the Apostles. When the multitudes gathered at Pentecost, *Then Peter said unto them, Repent, and be baptized every one of you in the name of Jesus Christ for the remission* (forgiveness) *of sins, and ye shall receive the gift of the Holy Ghost* [Acts 2:38].

Later, in the Book of Acts, Luke records what happened when Paul first . . . *came to Ephesus: and finding certain disciples, He said unto them, Have ye received* (Did you receive?) *the Holy Ghost since ye believed* [Acts 19:1-2a]? The disciples with whom Paul was speaking replied, . . . *We have not so much as heard whether there be any Holy Ghost* [Acts 19:2b].

After hearing their response, Paul's focus turned to baptism,

> *And he said unto them, Unto what then were ye baptized? And they said, Unto John's baptism.*
> *Then said Paul, John verily baptized with the baptism of repentance, saying unto the people, that they should believe on him which should come after him, that is, on Christ Jesus.*
> *When they heard this, they were baptized in the name of the Lord Jesus* [Acts 19:3-5].

Baptism represents a washing away of sins. However, it represents something even more important. They are baptized into the leadership of the Lord Jesus Christ. This is most important!

We are all familiar with the account of Moses leading the children of Israel out of Egypt and crossing over the Red Sea. Paul recounts this momentous event, saying to the Corinthians,

> *MOREOVER, brethren, I would not* (do not want) *that ye should be ignorant* (unaware), *how that all our fathers were under the cloud, and all passed through the sea;*
> *And were all baptized unto Moses in the cloud and in the sea* [1 Cor. 10:1-2].

This means that they were baptized into the leadership of Moses. They were baptized into Moses' guidance and ministry. The Israelites had become identified with Moses, with what he stood for, and with what he represented.

John Calvin proclaims two important truths regarding the baptism of professing Christians, declaring, "in baptism we are initiated into the teaching of Christ alone." Also, he stresses "that only His name is invoked, since baptism rests solely upon His power."

Baptism signifies our entering the realm under the influence of the Lord Jesus Christ. It means that formerly we belonged to the world, but now we do not.

When we are baptized, it means that we are confessing Christ and have announced that we are submitting ourselves to Him, we are going to follow Him, and He has become our Lord and Master.

The Israelites could have stayed in Egypt, but when they submitted themselves to Moses they followed his leadership.

All individuals who say they are *in Christ* are proclaiming that He and only He is their Lord and Master. This is easier said than done.

There are some things in which it is relatively easy to surrender to Christ and to acknowledge that He is the Lord and Master. There are other times it is difficult, especially when considering the things we covet, or when it comes to self.

Baptism signifies that we deny ourselves, take up His Cross, and follow Him. This results in unity with Christ, since it cannot produce division.

The *one baptism* leads to unity and is to be understood as a unity. This is the New Testament teaching which was adopted and supported by the Reformers. Any qualification or quantification of it is forbidden.

When a person is *in Christ* he is joined to Him, he has died with Him, he has been raised with Him, and he is a new creature. The person *in Christ* knows that his sins are forgiven. The person *in Christ* believes in the Lord Jesus Christ and believes that Christ died for his sins. More than that, he or she knows that the life of Christ is in him or her, that Christ is the Head of the body, and that he or she is a member of that body.

All this is true because he or she has been baptized into the one body of Christ by the Holy Spirit.

> *For by one Spirit are we all baptized into one body, whether we be Jews or Gentiles (Greeks), whether we be bond (slaves) or free; and have been all made to drink into one Spirit* [1 Cor. 12:13].

When realizing this and living accordingly there can be no division, there can only be unity.

Baptism has a special character. People want to establish limits, precise definitions, and interpretations. Fixing limits on baptism would be appropriate only if it were the means to an end and that was the only way to attain it, but then it would not be empowered by the Spirit and designated as a means for receiving the Spirit. It would become something placed in man's hands requiring a specific order and process with the attendant prerequisites and effects. It would become a thing. It would possibly deteriorate into something subject to manipulation and thereby lose the freedom of God moving over and through us by the Holy Spirit.

We have been stressing what baptism is not, but what is it in a positive sense? It is the self-manifestation of Jesus Christ, and we experience it in the power of the Holy Spirit. It is Christ who died and rose again. He cannot be divided. Interpreting baptism is as multifarious as the Christ-event in the New Testament.

How should the *one baptism* be understood?

First, it is an event that confronts man not only as a person, but in his individuality. The baptized person is given a name, a new name. A new person arises in witness to his or her faith and to the grace of God in Christ.

Second, baptism promises God's covenant with the baptized person and makes that person a partner to the covenant. It happens in such a way that the yes of the person is unconditional. However, that yes is not the power to enact or establish the covenant as God's yes is.

Third, baptism is a concrete, physical experience. The person experiences the indivisibility of God's covenant relationship and is to live in total subordination to God's leadership.

Fourth, baptism makes known the decision of God. His decision always precedes our willingness to believe.

Lastly, the unity of the community of believers is strengthened through baptism. *For as many of you as have been baptized into Christ have put on Christ* [Gal. 3:27].

The sole function of baptism is not to incorporate the person into the "body of the Church," but to signify this unity. Christ is the Head, we are the members. Christ is the leader, we are the followers and subject to His commands.

By virtue of baptism I become a member of the community of believers and am integrated into it. Then I can renounce my isolation or separation and turn to the One who is Lord. This occurs when we are baptized in the name of the Holy Trinity.

The New Testament evidence suggests that Christian baptism followed John's baptism of repentance and deliverance, adding to it union with Christ and admission to the community of believers. It was the means of entry into the church during the Apostolic Age. It was the means whereby the individual was united to Christ and received, among other benefits, the gift of the Holy Spirit.

The Apostle Paul, by saying *one baptism,* does not mean a rite or something magical. He means there is only one Lord who cleanses our soul (which the waters of baptism represent). The one Lord redeems us. He incorporates us into His body. We are to follow His leadership and to subordinate our wills to His will. He is to be our life, whereby we can say with Paul, *I live; yet not I, but Christ liveth in me* [Gal. 2:20]. The old self disappears, and the new self appears *in Christ. One Lord, one faith, one baptism* [Eph. 4:5].

Amen!

12

God the Father

> *There is one body, and one Spirit, even as ye are called in one hope of your calling;*
> *One Lord, one faith, one baptism,*
> *One God and Father of all, who is above all, and through all, and in you all* [Eph. 4:4–6].

It is important to remember that the fourth chapter is a continuation of the material presented in the first three chapters. It begins, *I therefore*. Paul laid the foundation by presenting and substantiating the doctrines imparted in the first three chapters.

Then he applies his teachings in a practical, explicit, and direct manner. His words should not be ignored or overlooked. They are like a sign post on the highway that arrests your attention and causes you to take action. It is the verbal causeway between the heavenly calling of the first three chapters and what our earthly conduct should be as described in the last three chapters.

Paul advises the Ephesians that they had passed from their old ways and conditions into a new life. They were now *in Christ*. This new position, this new relationship, demanded a severance from the old ways and ideas. Paul called them to a new walk, and they were to walk worthy of their new vocation. Then Paul with his invincible logic proceeds not only to call them, but to describe the different ways of walking that were to become part of their being. He was confronting them with a very significant fact. They had been transformed from being outside Christ to being *in Christ*. They had not been members of the community of believers; now they were. What is the difference? *The presence of Christ!*

Paul emphasizes an important truth in the first sixteen verses. It is unity, oneness. When we are *in Christ*, there is unity; when we are *in Christ*, there is oneness. Consequently, it is important when studying these verses and the magnificent truths contained in them that we understand why the Apostle stresses unity and oneness.

Please recall as we continue our journey through Ephesians,

> *Endeavoring to keep the unity of the spirit in the bond of peace.*
> *There is one body, and one spirit, . . . one hope of your calling.*
> *One Lord, one faith, one baptism,*
> *One God and Father of all, who is above all, and through all, and in you all* [Eph. 4:3–6].

This verse is the climax of the first six: first the Spirit, then the Son who brings us to the Father, and then God the Father.

Paul had the ability to rise to the occasion. In Romans, he provides a beautiful description of God and His ways, saying,

> *O the depth of the riches both of the wisdom and knowledge of God! how unsearchable are his judgments, and his ways past finding out!*
> FOR WHO HATH KNOWN THE MIND OF THE LORD? OR WHO HATH BEEN HIS COUNSELOR [Rom. 11:33–34]?

The Apostle never stops at the Spirit or the Son; he always goes to the Father.

Note how Paul presents the Spirit, the Son, and the Father in the fourth, fifth, and sixth verses of this chapter. This is also Peter's approach, who says clearly and concisely, *For Christ also hath once suffered for sins, the just for the unjust, that he might bring us to God, being put to death in the flesh, but quickened* (made alive) *by the Spirit* [1 Pet. 3:18].

Paul emphasizes that everything related to our salvation, or right relationship to God, suggests unity. This is clearly seen in the Holy Trinity. Each Person in the Trinity is concerned with our salvation and each One deals with a particular aspect of it. Each of the three cooperates and supports the other members of the Trinity.

In these three verses, the Apostle is getting the Ephesians to focus on the members of the Trinity, not on themselves. He does not want them to be subjective. He wants them to look to Christ and to God the Father. He wants them to realize that the Holy Trinity is concerned with their salvation and their relationship with Christ and with God.

The Apostle reveals that members of the community are in a positive relationship to the Spirit, the Son, and the Father, which makes unity inevitable. The way to attain and to maintain unity is to present the Gospel of Jesus Christ. It is not accomplished by setting up offices, or organizations, or committees. "Unity results from comprehending and understanding the truth," As wisely stated by Lloyd-Jones.

Paul's prayer in the third chapter includes this petition,

> *May be able to comprehend* (understand) *with all saints what is the breadth* (width), *and length, and depth, and height;*
> *And to know the love of Christ, which passeth knowledge, that ye might be filled with all the fullness of God* [Eph. 3:18–19].

It all ties together—the first, second, third, fourth, fifth, and sixth chapters of Ephesians. What thoughts and truths help us understand the principle of unity? The early Christians needed to understand there was only one God. The pagan world did not believe this nor do many people today. Paul taught throughout his ministry that there is only *One God*. Because there is only *One God*, there must be an essential unity among the followers. The Apostle affirms that there is one God, but three persons in the Godhead. We recognize the Spirit, Son, and Father and yet we say that the three are one God. It is taught throughout Scripture that the Spirit is in us, Christ is in us, and the Father is in us.

What is the objective of salvation? *To bring us to God!* It is not to bring us to Christ. The Lord Jesus Christ came into the world to bring us to God the Father. We come to our Father through the Lord Jesus Christ. What does Christ want to do? Bring us to God!

The message in the Bible reveals that God made man in His own image. However, sin and rebellion entered man's heart and mind, thereby separating him and us from God. It is God's plan of salvation that brings us back into a right relationship with Him. This message starts with God and returns us to God.

The great objective of salvation is not just to make us happy and to enable us to experience joy in our living though God's grace, but to reconcile us to God and to enjoy Him forever.

Those of us who are *in Christ* come together to the same God, and if we come to the same God there can be no divisions. The Apostle says, *For through him* (Christ) *we both* (Jew and Gentile) *have access by one Spirit unto the Father* [Eph. 2:18].

Previously the Jews had worshipped the one God, and the Gentiles had worshipped different pagan deities. Now that has changed, and both have access by one Spirit unto the Father. As Paul says, *One God and Father of all* [Eph. 4:6].

There are two questions to consider: What do we mean by God the Father? What does Paul mean by his statement? First, the former question. God discloses Himself unto us. He is always the loving God. He is holy, omnipotent, immutable, just, all-wise, gracious, merciful, and righteous.

God, as the Father, is always thought of in a certain way: His love is unconditional as manifested in His grace, His mercy, His faithfulness, and His patience. All these factors and attributes can be summarized with the words, God the Father.

The attributes ascribed to the Father make it clear that God's righteousness, wisdom, and holiness are inherent characteristics of His love, plus part and parcel of His grace, mercy, faithfulness, and patience. These are the attributes of the One God, who is our Father.

These attributes are expressed in the relationship between God the Father and His children. This is the relationship God has entered into with man.

What does the New Testament reveal about God the Father? Not that God is our Father, since it had been revealed in the Old Testament, but rather the essential character of the fatherhood of God. This revelation takes place and is evident in the Lord Jesus Christ.

Paul amplifies upon this, saying,

> *But when the fullness of the time was come, God sent forth his Son, made of a woman, made* (born) *under the law,*
> *To redeem them that were under the law, that we might receive the adoption of sons* [Gal. 4:4–5].

The law stands between the reality of sonship and the effective knowledge of God's fatherhood. Man as a servant, or bond slave, cannot know God as the Father. If the law has its effect, then the following must be true:

Man must know God as a partner in a relationship marked by "I give in order that you will give" or "God is viewed as a God of wrath." However, the significance of the New Testament is that the "sonship" of the true believers is real. And that God's fatherhood is true. How do these two things happen? They happen in the Lord Jesus Christ.

When we say that God's grace, mercy, faithfulness, and patience are attributes of God the Father, then we must show and recognize that these same inherent characteristics are real in the person of Jesus Christ.

Now consider the second question: what does Paul mean by the verse, *One God and Father of all, who is above all, and through all, and in you all* [Eph. 4:6]?

The word *all* appears four times. Of course, some jump to conclusions rather quickly. The word *all* used in this verse is in the masculine gender, not the neuter. What does this mean?

The Apostle is not saying, "One God and Father of all persons." What does he mean by this statement? Some say it means every single person and refers to the universal fatherhood of God. However, neither of those arguments is supported in the New Testament.

A careful analysis reveals that the aforementioned cannot be the proper interpretation. Earlier, it was stated that Scripture must be examined in its full context. The Apostle is writing about the church, the community of believers. He writes to the believers in Ephesus, not to the general population, saying, . . . *to the saints which are at Ephesus, and to the faithful in Christ Jesus* [Eph. 1:1].

He is not writing about the world. He is writing to those who belong to the body of Christ, to those who are *in Christ*. Paul writes to those who have been called and incorporated into the body of Christ.

The entire reference in this Scripture is to the people *in Christ* and to them only. The *all* covers these people only, and no one else.

Further proof of this thesis is contained in the last phrase of this verse, *and in you all*. This phrase is never used about the non-believer, nor the person outside Christ. God is only in the believer, the person who is *in Christ*. Further support for this position is found in the statement, *But unto everyone of us is given grace according to the measure of the gift of Christ* [Eph. 4:7].

Then in verses 8–16 of the fourth chapter, Paul proceeds to deal with the gifts provided to the members of the community and those things necessary for unity. The gifts God provided were *apostles, prophets, evangelists, pastors and teachers*. The purpose of the gifts was

> *For the perfecting* (equipping) *of the saints, for the work of the ministry, for the edifying of the body of Christ:*
> *Till we all come in* (into) *the unity of the faith, and of the knowledge of the Son of God, unto a perfect* (mature) *man, unto the measure of the stature of the fullness of Christ* [Eph. 4:12–13].

The reason for these gifts being

> *That we henceforth be no more children, tossed to and fro, and carried about with every wind of doctrine, by the sleight* (trickery) *of men, and cunning craftiness, whereby they lie in wait to deceive;*
>
> *But . . . may grow up into him in all things, which is the head, even Christ:*
>
> *. . .* (and) *maketh increase of the body unto the edifying of itself in love* [Eph. 4:14–16].

From the beginning of this chapter, the Apostle focuses attention on the body of Christ and its members. He is not directing anything to those on the outside. God is not the Father of all men.

> *Ye are of your father the devil, and the lusts* (desires) *of your father ye will do. He was a murderer from the beginning, and abode* (stands) *not in the truth, because there is no truth in him. When he speaketh a lie, he speaketh of his own* (from his own nature): *for he is a liar, and the father of it* [John 8:44].

Yes, God is the creator of all, but His fatherhood is limited to those who are *in Christ* and in the community of believers. The one truth we must grasp is that God is our Father.

We should be ever aware of what Peter said in affirming that we have become *partakers of the divine nature* [2 Pet. 1:4]. This does not mean we have become gods but that we have a principle of life, which comes from God Himself. When we receive this principle of life, we become "a child of God." God is our Father because when we are born of the Spirit, we are born of God, and we belong to the household of God. Paul says, *. . . ye are no more strangers and foreigners, but fellow citizens with the saints, and of the household of God* [Eph. 2:19].

When considering what Paul means, we must focus on unity and the term *one*. When we do, we can ask certain questions:

- Where does faith come from?
- Where does baptism come from?
- Where does the leadership, guidance, and discipline of Christ come from?
- Who brings about the unity?

God the Father is the answer. John Calvin affirms this statement by telling us that our heavenly Father "pours Himself forth to each of us and He gathers each of us to Himself."

Paul is not speaking of things universal. He is only speaking of the spiritual government pertaining to the true church, the community of believers, not to the secular world. God through the Holy Spirit pours Himself into all the members of the community. He embraces them and dwells in them. It is in this way we are united. This unity in the Spirit is seen in Jesus' prayer,

> *Holy Father, keep through thine own name those whom thou hast given me, that they may be one, as we are* [John 17:11].

> *For in him we live, and move, and have our being* [Acts 17:28].

We are to grasp these truths in their proper context.

Paul deals with the members of the community and has nothing to do with those outside Christ. He is concerned only with God's government and presence. It is for this reason he uses the term *Father*, which applies only to those who are *in Christ*.

Paul was a wise teacher. He knew his audience (and he knows us). Therefore, he continues this verse saying, *who is above all, and through all, and in you all* [Eph. 4:6]. He is working out the details.

There are misconceptions and misinterpretations as to what Paul is saying. Some interpret it to mean that the phrase *who is above all* refers to God and that *in you all* refers to the Spirit. However, that is not the proper exposition of this Scripture. Why? Because Paul has already dealt with the Spirit and the Lord Jesus Christ in verses 4 and 5. Now he is dealing with the Father.

What is Paul describing and to what is he referring? I suggest that he is thinking in terms of the community of believers. When he says *who is above all*, he is referring to the church or community, to those who have been redeemed, to those who are in the body of Christ and in this blessed unity. God the Father is the One who originated the idea. The church or community is His grand design.

God hath blessed us in Christ. God hath adopted us as His children *in Christ* unto Himself. God the Father is the One who is above all. Paul reminds us of these truths as he deals with the questions of unity and oneness. It is God's plan and eternal purpose to reunite, to gather together in one all things *in Christ*.

Next, Paul says God is *through all*. What does he mean? He is saying that God permeates the whole life of the community and sustains that life. God brought the church or community into being. He keeps it in being, and He will continue to keep it.

Recall Paul's prayer at the close of the first chapter, where he beseeches God that

> *The eyes of your understanding being enlightened; that ye may know what is the hope of his calling, and what the riches of the glory of his inheritance in the saints;*
> *... the exceeding greatness of His power to us-ward who believe; ...*
> *Which he wrought in Christ* [Eph. 1:18–20].

Immediately following this prayer, Paul says to the Ephesian believers, *AND you hath he quickened* (made alive), *who were dead in trespasses and sins* [Eph. 2:1]. It is God the Father, *who is rich in mercy*, that did this.

Perhaps God's mercy and grace is best summarized in Philippians.

> *Wherefore, my beloved, as ye have always obeyed, not as in my presence only, but now much more in my absence, work out your own salvation with fear and trembling.*
> *For it is God which worketh in you both to will and to do of* (according to) *his good pleasure* [Phil. 2:12–13].

God is *above all* and He is *through all*.

Third and last, but just as important, God is *in you all*. This means that God the Father, God the Son, and God the Holy Spirit is in all the members of the community. *In whom ye also are builded* (being built) *together for a habitation of God through the Spirit* [Eph. 2:22]. The habitation is the community. God dwells in her and therefore in us. God makes His abode with us. This is seen in Jesus' words, *If a man love me, he will keep my words: and my Father will love him, and we will come unto him, and make our abode* (home) *with him* [John 14:23].

Therefore, is it any wonder that Paul states, *One God and Father of all, who is above all, and through all, and in you all* [Eph 4:6]?

Amen!

13

But Unto Every One

> *But unto every one of us is given grace according to the measure of the gift of Christ* [Eph. 4:7].

The Apostle introduces a subtle yet significant change in verse seven of the fourth chapter. During the first six verses he has been stressing unity and oneness. However, in the seventh verse Paul says, *But unto everyone of us is given grace according to the measure of the gift of Christ.* What does this mean? What does it signify? What about the words unity, unison, and uniformity? They do not all mean the same thing. Therefore, once again we come face-to-face with that old bugaboo: What does our mindset say compared to what Scripture says?

This verse begins with the word *But*. What does that do? It refers us back to the previous verses and thoughts. When we read the seventh verse we should proceed to read verses eleven to sixteen.

The Apostle in verses four, five, and six establishes the great principle of unity and then in verse seven says, *But unto everyone of us.* He is not shattering unity; he does not want us to lose our identity; and he knows we are still individuals.

The explanation is we are one *in Christ*. We are members of *one body*. But we are different members of the same body. We have all been saved the same way. Regeneration in each of us is by the same Spirit. We are all members of the household of God.

Our unity does not mean that we are identical, that we are exactly the same in every respect. No, no, no, and again no! It is in this way that the Apostle introduces diversity, differences, variety, and variations.

It is interesting to note that there is diversity in unity and unity in diversity. Essentially, we are one, but in many respects we differ. Also, we need to recognize and to accept the fact that the diversity does not break the unity and the unity does not eliminate the diversity.

A question to consider is: How can this great unity, which Paul emphasizes, be preserved in view of diversity and variety? The body of Christ, the community of believers, is characterized by unity and diversity. How are they held together?

The controlling principle in all this is the Lord Jesus Christ. He is the Head of the body or the community, and He is the giver of the various gifts enjoyed by the individual members. This is what assures unity in diversity and diversity in unity. The Lord Jesus Christ gives the Spirit and through the Spirit gives His gifts. We have different gifts but one Lord.

The word *But* at the beginning of the seventh verse "should arrest our attention. It denotes an abrupt change in thought," according to Ruth Paxson. You will recall, *Blessed be the God and Father of our Lord Jesus Christ, who hath blessed us with all spiritual blessings in heavenly places in Christ* [Eph. 1:3]. The spiritual blessings were and are given to those who are *in Christ* and members of the community.

Paul talks about the gifts given *in Christ*. Ruth Paxson amplifies upon this with an interesting, truthful, description, saying there is "a divinely determined-diversity in the divinely purposed unity in the body of Christ."

Remember, Christ is the Head of the body. He selects members of the community to receive specific gifts. These gifts are given so that the individuals may participate and share in the extension and edification of the body.

God bestows these diverse gifts upon members so as to join together their various gifts for a common purpose. Think, if you will, of an orchestra or chorus. They join together for a common purpose. A certain measure is allotted to each person, but no one receives a portion that allows him or her to be self-sufficient or to be self-satisfied with his or her own gifts. It is only by communicating and working with one another that they have the ability to utilize their talents to the fullest.

John Calvin accurately states, "On no one has God bestowed all things, but each has received a certain measure, so that we need one another; and by bringing together what is given to them individually, they help one another." Think on that!

The Apostle uses the words *grace* and *gift* in this seventh verse. In so doing he reminds us that whatever gifts we possess are bestowed by the grace of God, and they are given unto us. Therefore, we should not be proud of them. To the contrary, we should realize we are under a deeper obligation to God and give Him thanks upon thanks.

He bestows upon each member the gift or gifts that a person needs in order to accomplish the tasks that he is to do. Each one has a gift, though it may differ in quality, quantity, and type. Yet it is to be used for the benefit and blessing of all members of the community.

Consider what Paul says in culminating this portion of Scripture, *From whom the whole body fitly joined together and compacted* (knit together) *by that which every joint supplieth, according to the effectual* (effective) *working in the measure of* (each part doing its share) *every part, maketh increase* (causes growth) *of the body unto the edifying of itself in love* [Eph. 4:16].

We are to realize that no matter how insignificant, weak, or obscure we may consider ourselves as members of Christ's body, we are important and have something to contribute to the functioning and spiritual health of that body. If we feel we have received strength, then how much more we need support from others.

The gifts bestowed on each member are given in order to increase and build up the community for the glory of God. Each of us should know what gifts we have received. We should value them as special gifts from Christ Himself. Therefore, they are to be used to serve Him.

What is the purpose of bestowing gifts upon the members of the community? It is to carry out the sovereign, eternal purpose of God in Christ Jesus. How is this revealed? It is shown in:

> *For the perfecting* (equipping) *of the saints, for the work of the ministry, for the edifying of the body of Christ* [Eph 4:12]. The little word *for* indicates it is a current and continuing process that never ends.
>
> *Till we all come in* (into) *the unity of the faith, and of the knowledge of the Son of God, unto a perfect* (mature) *man, unto the measure of the stature of the fullness of Christ* [Eph. 4:13]. The word *till* suggests the working out of a predestined purpose. And what a glorious purpose it is!
>
> *That we henceforth be no more children, tossed to and fro, and carried about with every wind of doctrine, by the sleight* (trickery) *of men, and cunning craftiness, whereby they lie in wait to deceive* [Eph. 4:14].

The word *henceforth* tells us that we are no longer children in the faith and that we are to grow up as members of Christ's body.

When considering Paul's statements in this portion of Scripture, one should realize that God is not working in a haphazard manner. He is proceeding toward the ultimate goal He has purposed for the community, which is the fullness of Christ. Therefore, as members of Christ's body we are to pursue the following requirements: steady, progressive growth from spiritual infancy to spiritual maturity; growth *in Christ*; and grow *unto a perfect* (mature) *man, unto the measure of the stature of the fullness of Christ* [Eph. 4:13]. This sounds somewhere between the ludicrous and the impossible, yet there it is! The standard for the community of believers has been established.

It is our responsibility to discover the standards and requirements that have been established, to accept them, and to adjust our lives so that we may not only pursue them, but achieve them. This is important and bears repeating.

- We are to discover the truths presented and established by God in Christ,
- we are to accept them, and
- we are to achieve them, with God's help.

How often we want to say God's standards are too high, or they are impracticable, or impossible in today's world or in our particular circumstances. Therefore, we want God to lower His standards or expectations.

However, He will not do that! He is determined to bring our performance and standards up to His level.

In order to accomplish His purpose, God provides and bestows special gifts upon some members of the body so they may be used to prepare each member for his or her task.

It is time to remind ourselves of our initial question. How can this great unity, which Paul emphasizes, be preserved in view of diversity and variety?

Paul says to the Corinthians,

> *Now there are diversities* (various kinds) *of gifts, but the same Spirit.*
> *And there are differences of administrations* (ministries), *but the same Lord.*

> *And there are diversities of operations* (activities), *but it is the same God which worketh all in all* (all things).
> *But the manifestation of the Spirit is given to every man to profit withal* (all) *[1 Cor. 12:4–7].*
>
> *But all these worketh that one and the self-same Spirit, dividing* (distributing*) to every man severally* (individually) *as he will* [1 Cor. 12:11].

The harmony of the community resides in the fact that there is unity in many parts. The different gifts are all directed to the same end. As the fourth verse above states, *there are diversities* (various kinds) *of gifts* and they are distinguished from one another, but they are combined together and function in unity.

Paul urges the followers to be content with their gifts and to make the most of them. He encourages them to share their gifts. He instructs them to bring what they have and not to keep their gifts to themselves. He wants them to work together harmoniously for the edification and upbuilding of everyone in the community of believers.

Paul reveals in the seventh verse above how God wants the gifts used. He does not bestow them on people for nothing. He does not intend the gifts to be used frivolously, or merely for show. The reason He bestows the gifts is to benefit the church, Christ's body.

When a gift is bestowed it is for the purpose of unlocking certain treasures and revealing them. And, to allow one to receive a better interpretation.

Paul calls the Corinthians back to unity. He reminds them that whatever they have obtained, whatever gifts they have, they all come from one source. Each person needs the help of others.

The Spirit distributes the gifts among the members of the community. Why? So that each one may make a contribution to the common good. God wants us dependent one upon another. Paul urges the believers to bond themselves together for the benefit of each other. He wants them to pool their gifts. Why? Because the gifts were given to them by God so that they might help one another.

The Apostle in 1 Corinthians points out that even though there are different members performing different functions they are all connected together to form a basic unity. Therefore, we are to be concerned about our unity with each other as well as our unity with Christ.

Christ invests us with a very high honor. He wants us to be recognized as members of His body. As Paul says, the church . . . *is his body, the fullness of him that filleth all in all* [Eph. 1:23]. Christ does not want to be separated from His members. As St. Augustine stated and then exclaimed with a mischievous sense of humor, "since in Christ we are a fruitful vine, out of Christ what are we but withered little branches." There is unity in diversity and there is diversity in unity, but it occurs in Christ.

After writing verse seven, the Apostle could have proceeded to the eleventh verse. However, he does not. He inserts the thoughts contained in verses eight, nine, and ten. This is something Paul was prone to do. He has a definite thought in mind, and then he appears to digress as he says,

> *For to one is given by the Spirit the word of wisdom; to another the word of knowledge by the same Spirit;*
> *To another faith by the same Spirit; to another the gifts of healing by the same Spirit;*
> *To another the working of miracles; to another prophecy; to another discerning of spirits; to another divers kinds of tongues; to another the interpretation of tongues* [1 Cor. 12:8–10].

In this instance, there is a definite reason for inserting these three verses.

Paul uses the phrase *Wherefore he saith* to begin verse 8 of the fourth chapter of Ephesians. He uses the eighth verse to remind the hearers that God's grace and gifts had been foretold. Then he proceeds to quote from the Sixty-eighth Psalm.

Paul's message is that the grace and gifts given to the members at Ephesus are not to be thought of as something new or something that occurred to God only recently. On the contrary, he points out that it was always part of God's purpose and His plan of redemption. By referring to the Sixty-eighth Psalm, he shows that God had revealed it centuries before. David praises God, saying,

> *Sing unto God, sing praises to his name: extol* (praise) *him that rideth upon the heavens* (deserts) *by his name JAH* (Lord)*, and rejoice before him.*
> *A father of the fatherless, and a judge* (defender) *of the widows, is God in his holy habitation* [Ps. 68:4–5].

In this psalm, David extols the name of God. He does so because of the great victory which God had given him. It reminded him of the victory God had given the Israelites when they were coming out of Egypt. David reminds the Israelites that all these victories were the victories of God. Paul ascribes it all to the Lord Jesus Christ. He is referring to the gift of Christ.

> *Thou hast ascended on high, thou hast led captivity captive: thou hast received gifts for* (among) *men; yea, for the rebellious also, that the Lord God might dwell among them.*
> *Blessed be the Lord, who daily loadeth us with benefits, even the God of our salvation* [Ps. 68:18–19].

Of course, there is a question at this point: what were David and Paul talking about? The psalmist is talking about Jehovah, Jah (Lord). The Apostle is talking about the Lord Jesus Christ. How do we reconcile these things?

We are to bear in mind the following when reading Scripture: often there is a double meaning in the Old Testament. It is true in the Psalms and with the prophets. This fact is revealed as David writes what we identify as the Sixty-eighth Psalm, saying, *Thou hast ascended on high, thou hast led captivity captive* [Ps. 68:18].

He writes about an historical event. He focuses on God and praises Him. Because he is under the influence of the Holy Spirit, he is also led to write about things beyond the present time. The Holy Spirit led David to describe a past and present circumstance in such a way as to foreshadow what was going to happen later. Therefore, David was able to give an accurate description of what happened in and through the Lord Jesus Christ.

Paul recognized that David, in writing this psalm, was citing all the victories which God had wrought for the salvation of His people, the community of believers. Therefore, he properly applies this verse about the ascension of God to the person of Jesus Christ.

John Calvin, inspired by the Holy Spirit, provides assurance, joy, and contentment with these stirring, strengthening, and stalwart words for the believers, "The greatest triumph, which God ever won, was when Christ, after subduing sin, conquering death, and putting Satan to flight rose majestically to heaven, that He might exercise His glorious reign over the church."

David contemplated the glory of God in the continuing existence of His church. However, there was no ascension more memorable than when Christ was raised to the right hand of God. Some authorities say the Jah that David writes about is the Lord Jesus Christ.

Why is this so? You cannot say that God the Father received gifts for men. You cannot say of the Father that He ascended, because He has always been in heaven, and He will always be. There is only One of whom it can be said, He ascended, and that is Christ.

Again, we find the Doctrine of the Holy Trinity, the Spirit leading us to Christ; Christ subordinating Himself for the work of salvation and bringing us to the Father; and the Father wanting us to be reconciled.

Now let us turn to the Sixty-eighth Psalm, verse 18 and compare it with Ephesians 4:8.

> *Thou hast ascended on high, thou hast led captivity captive: thou hast received gifts for* (among) *men; yea, for the rebellious also, that the Lord God might dwell among them* [Ps. 68:18].

> *Wherefore he saith,* WHEN HE ASCENDED UP ON HIGH, HE LED CAPTIVITY CAPTIVE, AND GAVE GIFTS UNTO MEN [Eph. 4:8].

It is true of the Lord Jesus Christ that He both received and he gave. It is all one action. The same Person receives and at the same moment He gives.

The gifts that come to the church of the true believers come from and through the Lord Jesus Christ. In one instance He emphasizes that it is the Father who gives them to the Son, and in the other instance He emphasizes it is the Son who gives them to the individual members of the community. The Son receives in order to give.

Paul wants to show in these verses that there is unity in diversity, and diversity in unity; Christ ascended, and the ascension of God in the Person of Jesus Christ was far greater than the ancient triumphs of the Church; Christ is the giver of all gifts; Christ receives in order to give; and all gifts come from Him and they always will!

Where then is thy boasting?

Amen!

14

Worship Intelligently

> *And he* (himself) *gave some, apostles, and some, prophets; and some, evangelists; and some, pastors and teachers;*
> *For the perfecting* (equipping) *of the saints, for the work of the ministry, for the edifying of the body of Christ* [Eph. 4:11–12].

One truth having an impact upon each of us is our individual responsibility to worship intelligently. God has blessed us with spiritual blessings and He has *given grace according to the measure of the gift of Christ* [Eph. 4:7]. He has provided us with the mental capabilities to learn, to acquire knowledge, to understand, and to persevere.

Previously, we considered one Spirit, one Lord, one faith, and one baptism, then one God and Father of all. After that we focused attention on ourselves, and on unity in diversity and diversity in unity.

Much information has been presented and examined about the Lord Jesus Christ. Paul has presented a wealth of material about Him in the hope that we will *walk* more closely with Him during the days allotted to us. This *walk* is to be a *walk* in unity, holiness, love, light, wisdom, praise, and harmony.

These factors are the elements of our *walk*. They are to become part of us. They are to be in us just as much as our muscles, blood, and mind. However, if they are to be part of us, then we must realize we are part of the body of Christ, and we are to *walk* with Him. We are to use our minds and mental capabilities to the fullest. We are to embrace the Word of God, the life of Christ, and the power of the Holy Spirit, not ignore them. Paul tells us to

Let this mind be in you, which was also in Christ Jesus [Phil. 2:5].

Think of that! What does it mean? Literally, "keep thinking this." It is a command to live in harmony with others. We are not to exhibit selfish ambition, but we are to share the values revealed to us by Christ, have unity in the Spirit, and be concerned about the needs and problems of other community members.

Paul wants us to imitate Christ, to be obedient unto Him, and to have the same attitude that was *in Christ*, which consisted of humbling Himself, yielding voluntarily, considering God's will first and foremost, emptying Himself, having no pride, and being anything but self-centered.

He did all these things and more. Yet originally He was in the form of God. He did not manifest Himself to be what He was, nor did He openly assume or proclaim in the view of men what was His by all rights. He became a servant in the truest sense of the word. He was obedient in every facet of His earthly life and ministry.

What are we to do? Worship God! Learn about Him through the study of His Word. Pray that the Holy Spirit will reveal His will and enlighten us as we walk with Christ and endeavor to glorify the Father. What did Christ do?

- He went about His Father's business;
- He was tempted in the wilderness;
- He was challenged, ridiculed, and confronted by the Pharisees, scribes, and Sadducees;
- He was betrayed, He suffered under Pontius Pilate, and He was taken to Calvary's Hill; and
- He was crucified, bled, and died.

Yet He was never defeated. Through it all, He was victorious.

O DEATH, WHERE IS THY STING? O GRAVE (HADES), WHERE IS THY VICTORY [1 Cor. 15:55]?

But thanks be to God, which giveth us the victory through our Lord Jesus Christ.
Therefore, . . . be ye steadfast, unmovable, always abounding in the work of the Lord, . . . (and) *know that your labor is not in vain* (futile) *in the Lord* [1 Cor. 15:57–58].

We must understand that Christ in His own person destroyed sin. In so doing, He met the requirements of the law; He endured the curse; He satisfied the wrath of God; He procured life; He made us heirs, joint heirs; and He enabled us to share in God's blessings and to receive His gifts.

Further, there are several points to remember, as we continue to progress:

- Christ and Christ alone is Head of the church.
- The church, His body, consists of many members, each having its own function under the Head.
- We are to discover what our mission is and assume responsibility for discharging it.
- *Unto every one of us is given grace according to the measure of the gift of Christ* [Eph. 4:7].
- *He* (Himself) *gave some, apostles; and some, prophets; and some, evangelists; and some, pastors and teachers* [Eph. 4:11]. The Greek word for *He* in this verse is *autos*. It means, "He Himself." Therefore, this verse should read "He Himself gave some...."

It is the Lord Jesus Christ who gives. Remember this.

We are to know the things we have been talking about. We are to know Scripture. What happens when we do not?

Divisions, schisms, jealousy, envy, strife, rivalry, heartbreak, confusion, false ideas and practices, and the inability to walk with the Lord Jesus Christ become evident in our lives, resulting in our not being able to *walk worthy of the vocation* (calling) *wherewith ye are called*.

Who is to know Scripture? All the members of Christ's body. Not just a few. Not just the apostles, or pastors, or preachers, or teachers, neither the old nor the young, but all the members. Everyone is to know the biblical teachings concerning the body of Christ. We are all to learn, to know, and to practice.

What did our Lord do in order that we might learn, know, and practice? Christ is the giver of every good gift to what we call the church, but which is in reality the body of Christ. He gave unto the early church some to be apostles and prophets. This was the foundation with Jesus Christ Himself being the chief cornerstone and to it were added living stones, one by one. This required evangelists who could go far and wide, and proclaim the Gospel. They were also to extend the boundaries of the church. They were to win souls and to add to Christ's body one by one. When individuals were added, they needed to be shepherded and tended to, so there was a need for pastors. Then there was a need for the members of the body to increase their knowledge of Christ through the Word. Therefore, there was the need for teachers. The evangelist labors to extend the church while the pastor and teacher are required to nurture and to edify the body.

These various gifts are bestowed with a definite, divine purpose. It should be pointed out and emphasized that no gift is given for the sake of the person on whom it is bestowed. The gifts are given for the whole community.

The pastor and teacher are not commissioned to do all the work. They are commissioned to feed, teach, and train the individual members so that each one may grow into spiritual maturity and be equipped to do his or her part in building up the whole body.

We have no right to remain babes *in Christ*. We are to grow and become mature members of the body.

There are five offices enumerated in the eleventh verse. Three of these offices were temporary and certainly extraordinary: apostles, prophets, evangelists. The other two have been permanent: pastors and teachers.

We will examine each one. First, we look at the apostles. What were the distinguishing characteristics of the apostles? An apostle was:

- appointed by the Lord Jesus Christ;
- one who had seen the risen Lord and was a witness to His resurrection;
- one who had been commissioned by the Lord Himself, not by a church, or a delegation, or a group, or anyone else;
- one who had received a supernatural revelation of the truth;
- one who had received the power to speak with authority and infallibility; and
- one who had been given the power to work miracles.

Paul did not receive the Gospel from men. It was revealed to him by the Lord Jesus Christ.

> PAUL, an apostle, (not of men, neither by man, but by Jesus Christ, and God the Father, who raised him from the dead) [Gal. 1:1].
>
> For I neither received it of man, neither was I taught it, but by the revelation of Jesus Christ.
> But I certify (make known to) you, brethren, that the gospel which was preached of me is not after (according to) man [Gal. 1:11–12].

He was called on the road to Damascus; the risen Lord commissioned him, saying,

> ... I have appeared unto thee for this purpose, to make thee a minister and a witness both of these things which thou hast seen, and of those things in the which I will appear (reveal) unto thee [Acts 26:16].

He was Christ's ambassador and had unique authority. This explains why Paul could write to the Corinthians and Philippians and say, *be followers of me*. Paul knew that the words were not his own but those of the Lord Himself. This was neither egotism nor conceit on his part.

There have been no successors to the apostles.

Next, consider the prophets. The prophets differed from the apostles in that they did not have to see the risen Lord, spoke under the direct inspiration of the Holy Spirit, and included some women. *And there was one Anna, a prophetess* [Luke 2:36]. *And the same man had four daughters, virgins, which did prophesy* [Acts 21:9].

The prophets were people to whom the *truth* was imparted by the Holy Spirit. After receiving it, they received the power and wisdom to speak. When the New Testament was written, and made available, there was no longer a need for the direct revelation of the *truth*. The *truth* is in Scripture.

The Spirit speaks to us through the Word. Therefore, there is no mention of the prophets in the later letters.

The revelation has been given. What we need now is illumination. We need the Holy Spirit to illuminate the Word, to grant unto us understanding. We should pray for illumination and understanding as Paul did in his prayers in the first and third chapters of this letter.

Evangelists were the ones who announced good tidings. The evangelist in the New Testament was someone who had been given a special ability and power to make known the facts of the Gospel of our Lord

Jesus Christ. Usually they were appointed by the apostles. They were sent to do specific chores. Sometimes they preceded the apostles, but usually they followed them.

Timothy and Titus were evangelists. Paul reminded Timothy to do the work of an evangelist, saying, *Watch thou in all things, endure afflictions, do the work of an evangelist, make full proof of thy ministry* [2 Tim. 4:5].

The evangelists worked closely with the apostles. They had not seen the risen Lord. However, they were individuals the Holy Spirit called through the apostles.

The evangelists received certain gifts which were knowing Jesus' ministry and Scripture; having the ability to present the Gospel clearly and precisely; having authority and power from the Holy Spirit; and possessing spiritual fervor in proclaiming the Gospel. God raises up evangelists for a specific purpose, which is "to restore pure doctrine to its lost position," because it is always needed according to Calvin.

And now to the offices of pastors and teachers. There is a slight difference in the wording for pastors and teachers. It says *some, pastors and teachers*. This has resulted in two points of view among the scholars. Some say that this clearly denotes only one office. Others say that there are two offices.

However, as John Calvin wisely points out through his insightful observations, "teaching is the duty of all pastors; but there is a particular gift of interpreting scripture, so that sound doctrine may be kept and a man may be doctor (teacher) who is not fitted to preach."

Pastors are those to whom is committed the care and responsibility of a particular flock. Sometimes the pastors will also be teachers, but the duties are different.

The pastor is concerned with the government and direction of his flock, as well as the instruction and rule of it. Also, he is to be the guardian, custodian, protector, and director of it.

The teacher, whether he be the pastor or another, has the responsibility to provide instruction in the doctrine and truth as it is found and revealed in the Lord Jesus Christ.

A pastor or teacher should never claim to have received a revelation. The only claim people performing these necessary functions can make is that they read the Word, study, pray, and believe the Holy Spirit enlightens them with understanding.

These last two offices generally go together in a pastor. Also, they are the two perpetual offices, provided for our edification, enlightenment, and growth as members of Christ's body.

Why did the Lord Jesus Christ give *some, apostles; and some, prophets; and some, evangelists; and some, pastors and teachers*? For the perfecting of the saints; for edifying the body of Christ; to come in the unity of the faith; for knowledge of the Son of God; to be no more children, but to become mature in the faith; and to know the doctrine and truth of Jesus Christ. Who called these people? The Lord Jesus Christ. Paul states it clearly and succinctly with these memorable words: *And are built on the foundation of the apostles and prophets, Jesus Christ himself being the chief corner stone* [Eph. 2:20].

The apostles were to publish and proclaim the gospel throughout the world, to plant churches, and to establish the kingdom of Christ. They were itinerant. They had no churches committed to them.

The prophets were to interpret prophecies and to foretell as it was related to the proclamation of the Word and the teachings of Christ during His earthly ministry.

The evangelists were to continue feeding and watering the flock.

The pastors and teachers are to present and interpret Scripture, by the power of the Holy Spirit.

Why were these gifts given? That we might know Christ and God the Father, worship intelligently, walk with Christ, grow in the faith, do as He would have us to do, and glorify God.

The gifts were also given as Paul states, *"For the perfecting* (equipping) *of the saints.* The special gifts are bestowed with a definite, divine design. No gift is bestowed for the sake of the man himself. It is given to one for the sake of the whole. Neither does it place the monopoly of service in the hands of a gifted few. The evangelist, pastor and teacher are not commissioned by the Lord to do all the work of the church, but rather to so feed, teach and train the saints individually that each of them be brought to spiritual maturity and thoroughly equipped to fill his place and do his work in building up the whole body. Every Christian had been made a king and priest unto God (Rev. 1:6). As the whole body is bound together in faith and in life, so is it also united in service.

"In Ephesians God has shown us what is our responsibility in this matter of keeping this God-ordained and God-designed unity of the spirit in the Body of Christ. We should have a fixed determination that we shall not allow anything for which we are to blame to separate us even a hairs-breadth from any other member of the Body. We should study diligently how to keep this unity; and make it our personal business to advocate and advance it whenever possible. We should determine to stand together on the basis of truth and in the bond of love as an act of allegiance and devotion to Him who is our Lord, and thus glorify Him by walking in unity," as beautifully and forcefully stated by Ruth Paxson.

These are our responsibilities in serving Him each and every day as His disciples while faithfully fulfilling our obligations.

Amen!

15

Faith and Knowledge

> *Till we all come in* (into) *the unity of the faith, and of the knowledge of the Son of God, unto a perfect* (mature) *man, unto the measure of the stature of the fullness of Christ* [Eph. 4:13].

The thirteenth verse of this fourth chapter is a watershed. The Apostle refers to the vast amount of information presented up to this point in Ephesians, especially in this portion of the fourth chapter, and prepares the way for applying these truths in the remaining passages of this holy epistle.

Paul and scholars since his time believe that nothing is more important than to understand the concept of the church as we call it, or the body of Christ as may be more appropriate.

Our failure to understand what membership in the body of Christ means, the dignity, privilege, and responsibility of it, is what causes most of the difficulties we encounter. We need to experience and recapture the New Testament teachings concerning His body and seeing ourselves as members of it.

This focal verse is not meant to be repetitious, but to emphasize the truths preceding and following it, which is a strong link in this vital chain.

Ephesians says more about the church, the body of Christ, than any other portion of the New Testament. This fourth chapter devotes more attention to the church's existence and function than any other section of this letter. Paul urges the saints to be humble, united, and strong in mutual love and in the bond of peace. However, as was his custom he could never go very long without talking about the Lord Jesus Christ. He urges us to do things and then gives the reason for so doing, saying,

> *But now in Christ Jesus ye who sometimes* (once) *were far off are made nigh by the blood of Christ.*
>
> *For he* (himself) *is our peace, who hath made both one, and hath broken down the middle wall of partition* (division) *between us;*
>
> *Having abolished in his flesh the enmity, even the law of commandments contained in ordinances; for to make* (create) *in himself of twain* (the two) *one new man, so making peace;*
>
> *And that he might reconcile both unto God in one body by the cross, having slain* (put to death) *the enmity thereby:*
>
> *And came and preached peace to you which were afar off, and to them that were nigh* [Eph. 2:13–17].

Verses 4–6 of the fourth chapter "combine distinctly Christian creedal elements," according to Markus Barth. The creed speaks of a oneness exerting a unifying force within and throughout the community of saints. Paul amplifies on this in the following verses:

- . . . *ye are* called in one hope of your calling;
- the *one body* is growing;
- the *one baptism* declares and confesses the sin which plagues the church, and claims the promises God makes available;
- the *One God and Father . . . who is above all, and through all, and in you all* is the same to those who have believed, do believe, and will believe;
- verses 7–10 describe the various gifts given by our Lord Jesus Christ, *that he might fill all things;*
- verse 11 describes the gifts given to some for proclaiming the Word of God, and for growing and building up the body of Christ;
- verses 12–14 explain that the gifts were given to prepare the saints for their ministry; prepare them to meet the Lord Jesus Christ; and to protect them from being tossed to and fro, and from being deceived by cunning craftiness; and
- verses 15–16 state that we may grow into Him, even Christ, and that we will be fitly joined together in His body
  [Selections from Eph. 4:4–16].

The ultimate objective is that the saints, you and me, be made perfect. The people of God cannot be made perfect nor live as they should without the Head, Jesus Christ. The real mark of the living body of Christ is one of unity and continuous change in order to be conformed to Him, Christ Jesus, who is greater than the church.

It is Christ that brings the members of His body, the church, "into a harmonious relationship with one another . . . Christ joins believers together and unites them by the divinely ordained ministries of Christians who possess diverse spiritual gifts, which are exercised and used among believers for the common good. The church's spiritual growth . . . comes from Christ through the believers' ministry to one another as they employ their spiritual gifts," as appropriately described in *The King James Bible Study*.

These truths penned by the Apostle describe a loving, humble church that responds to her tasks and is eager to reach the goal established by the Lord. The church described by Paul does not even begin to pretend to possess, master, or administer the Lord and his gifts. She is meek and modest not only before the Lord, but before the nonbelievers.

The church, the members of Christ's body, promises to trust the Lord Jesus Christ, realizing they have a commitment to fulfill, recognizing they are to be obedient, and acknowledging that the ability to do these things is given, not self-generated.

The body of Christ and its members are nothing more, nothing less, than a joyful band of people moving forward to meet the Lord and their eyes are focused on Him.

However, the church will under no circumstances glorify herself at the expense of God! Her work is unfinished, and she is to show that she really is God's people by doing His will. The church is neither her own master, nor her own end. Beyond and above the church is God Himself and the Lord Jesus Christ who is Head of the body. Before proceeding consider,

> *Till we all come in* (into) *the unity of the faith, and of the knowledge of the Son of God, unto a perfect* (mature) *man, unto the measure of the stature of the fullness of Christ* [Eph. 4:13].

What stands out in this verse? The following:

- *Till we all come, in* (into) *the unity of the faith.*
- *Knowledge of the Son of God, unto a perfect man.*
- *The measure of the stature of the fullness of Christ.*

Calvin, the renowned theologian, shines additional light on these three truths proclaimed by the Apostle Paul. His words should be grasped and ingested since they provide nourishment for our faith and enable us to grow, and mature in it. *"Till we all come* . . . . He (Paul) had already said that the ministry of the Church is governed and ordered, so as to be perfect in every respect. Lest anyone should think that this necessary only for a single day, he tells them that it must be so right to the end. Or, to speak plainly, he tells us that the use of the ministry is not temporal, as if it were a preparatory school, but constant, so long as we live in this world. The enthusiasts dream that the ministry becomes useless, as soon as we have been led to Christ. The proud men, who want to know more than is proper, despise it as being childish and elementary. But Paul protests that we must persevere in this course till all our deficiencies are supplied; that is, that we must so progress till death under the mastership of Christ alone, that we are not ashamed to be the disciples of the Church, to which Christ has committed this duty.

"What follows, on *the knowledge of the Son of God*, I regard as an explanation. For the apostle wanted to explain what is the nature of true faith, and when it exists; that is, when the Son of God is known. For to Him alone faith ought to look, on Him depend, in Him to rest and terminate. If it tries to go farther, it will disappear, for it will no longer be faith, but a delusion. Let us remember that true faith is so contained in Christ, that it neither knows, nor desires to know, anything beyond Him.

"*Unto a perfect man*. This must read in opposition; as if he had said, 'What is the highest perfection of Christians? And why is this so?' Full manhood is in Christ. For foolish men do not seek their perfection in Christ as they should. It ought to be a principle among us, that everything outside Christ is hurtful and destructive. Whatever man is in Christ, he is, in every respect, perfect.

"*The age of fullness means full or mature age*. No mention is made of old age, for in this progress there is no place for it. Whatever grows old tends to decay; but the vigor of this spiritual life is continually growing."

The sagacious words of Paul and Calvin are as true today as they were when they were originally written. They are provided for our discernment, enlightenment, and strength. They are not to be discarded or ignored. They are to be a guiding light as we travel along life's pathway, because they will contribute to increasing our faith and to walking with the Lord Jesus as one of His disciples.

We are to come, all of us, to the very important, significant truths contained in this verse. When these things happen they both prepare and enable us to *walk worthy of the vocation* (calling) *wherewith ye are called* [Eph. 4:1]. Our walk is to be in unity, holiness, love, light, wisdom, praise, and harmony, even though we are in the world and confronted with trials, tribulations, and temptations. Remember, we are called to be witnesses. We are to attain two things: *unity of the faith* of the Son of God and *knowledge of the Son of God.*

The grammarian scholars agree that this verse should read, "Till we all come in (into) the unity of the faith of the Son of God, and of the knowledge of the Son of God." These two things come first, and they are followed by the phrase *unto a perfect* (mature) *man*. As usual, the Apostle is practical and places things in a specific order. The way to attain the perfection that Paul writes about is first to grasp the unity of the faith of the Son of God and to obtain knowledge of the Son of God.

What does Paul mean by *the unity of the faith*? Verse 5 says, *One Lord, one faith, one baptism.* Is there a contradiction between verse 5 and verse 13? No! In verse 5, we considered the *one faith* as being justification by faith only. Faith is the first step, and the *one faith* means we are justified by faith and only by faith.

It is the beginning but not the entire scope of the matter. It is the first step leading us forward in our relationship with Christ and to the time when there will be nothing lacking or missing from it.

These aspects of faith relative to the Son of God, about which there is a mystery, have resulted in disagreements among the followers of Christ. However, when we attain the perfection of our faith, we shall say and believe the same things, because at that time we shall know Him and see Him as He is.

This unity of faith is large and comprehensive. We cannot deal with it in an exhaustive manner here. However, there are certain important truths to consider and remember.

- Christ is the Son of God, and also the Son of man, whereby the unity of faith embraces both evenly, fifty/fifty. One is never emphasized over the other.
- Christ's eternal and unique deity cannot be over-emphasized, nor can his human nature, because He is truly man and He is truly God.

- In the beginning, God appointed His Son to be the heir of all things, including the people in His church.
- We are to read and study the four Gospels and the Epistles, to know Christ's teachings, and to consider Christ as the chief Priest.
- Christ offered Himself, He was obedient, He laid down His life, He sitteth on the right hand of the Father, and he is our Saviour.

This is all part of the unity of faith of the Son of God.

The Apostle also speaks of the knowledge of the Son of God. It appears the Apostle is referring to something additional when he says *and of the knowledge of the Son of God.*

Faith leads to knowledge, and there is an element of knowledge in faith. Differentiating between these two things is difficult. However, we must endeavor to do so. You can have faith without having a particular knowledge or without having much knowledge, but you cannot have faith without having a certain knowledge. You cannot believe the things to which we have been referring without knowing something about them.

The Greek word for knowledge used in this thirteenth verse is *epignōsis*. It is a strong word and means "all knowledge." This is something that is over and above intellectual knowledge or apprehension. It is deeper and more profound.

A vital part of preaching and teaching is to bring us to a fuller, more complete knowledge. It is an essential part of building up the body of Christ. We are to come to the knowledge of the Son of God.

Paul had known of justification by faith and of righteousness after the law as well as righteousness that is from God by faith. However, the Apostle still had one great yearning and that was to know Him, to know His sufferings, the power of His Resurrection, and Christ Himself. Paul's prayer at the end of the third chapter is compelling when he petitions,

> ... *the Father of our Lord Jesus Christ,* ... [Eph. 3:14].

> *That Christ may dwell in your hearts by faith; that ye, being rooted and grounded in love,*
> *May be able to comprehend* (understand) *with all saints what is the breadth* (width), *and length, and depth, and height;*
> *And to know the love of Christ, which passeth knowledge, that ye might be filled with all the fullness of God* [Eph. 3:17–19].

The knowledge about which the Apostle speaks is knowing His personal love for us; knowing Him directly; knowing that our communion and fellowship is with Him; knowing that we are the branches and He is the vine; and knowing that we receive His power, strength, and grace in His fullness. The Apostle John adds clarity and emphasis to these truths that hit us right between the eyes when he says, as revealed to him by the Holy Spirit,

> *He came unto his own, and his own received him not.*
> *But as many as received him, to them gave he power* (the right) *to become the sons* (children) *of God, even to them that believe on his name:*
> *Which were born, not of blood, nor of the will of the flesh, nor of the will of man, but of God.*
> *And the Word was* (became flesh) *made flesh, and dwelt among us, . . . full of grace and truth* [John 1:11–14].
>
> *And of his fullness have all we received, and grace for grace* [John 1:16].

The Holy Spirit through the Apostle John wants us to grasp, understand, and accept the truth that Christ dwelt among us not only for us to behold His glory, but that He was and is *full of grace and truth*. Not only that, but we have received, we are receiving, and we will continue to receive *of his fullness . . .* and *grace for grace*. We are to accept these truths with assurance.

To know these truths requires certain things. Consider the encounter between the woman from Samaria and Jesus at Jacob's well. She was there for refreshing water from the deep well when Jesus said to her that *he would have given thee living water* [John 4:10]. This caused her to ask,

> *Art thou greater than our father Jacob . . . ?*
> *Jesus answered, . . . Whosoever drinketh of this water shall thirst again:*
> *But whosoever drinketh of the water that I shall give him shall never thirst; but the water I shall give him shall be in him a well* (fountain) *of water springing up into everlasting life* [John 4:12–14].

We are to drink continuously of the living water.

We are to receive, we are to eat and drink, then we are to receive, and we are to eat and drink, again and again, if we are to have this knowledge of the Son of God bestowed upon us. We are to attain unto . . . *the unity of the faith and of the knowledge of the Son of God, unto a perfect* (mature) *man* [Eph. 4:13].

The body of Christ is to grow in faith, love, and knowledge. Paul says, we

> *. . . do not cease to pray for you, and to desire that ye might be filled with the knowledge of his will in all wisdom and spiritual understanding;*
> *That ye might walk worthy of the Lord unto all pleasing, being fruitful in every good work, and increasing in the knowledge of God* [Col. 1:9-10].

We are to increase in knowledge and to bear fruit, much fruit.

However, the unity and knowledge we receive depends upon the faith, obedience, and selflessness of Christ. The way for us to grow is to have faith in Him and knowledge of Him. Faith and knowledge go together. Faith alone may puff us up, and there is knowledge that puffs up, but love edifies.

We are to spend time with the teachings of Christ contained in the New Testament. The illumination provided in the Word and by the Holy Spirit will enable us to understand it. We are to be diligent in studying Scripture. It is the responsibility of the pastors and teachers to inform the people about these things and to assist in building them up.

The objective is twofold: unity of the faith of the Son of God, and knowledge of the Son of God. Why? So that we may know Him personally, subjectively, and experientially, and so that we may rejoice in knowing Him and walking with Him.

What follows *the unity of faith, and knowledge of the Son of God?* . . . *unto a perfect* (mature) *man, unto the measure of the stature of the fullness of Christ* [Eph. 4:13]? The perfect man means Christ and His church. He is the Head and the members are the different parts of His body. Thus, the perfect man can be regarded as the Church in a perfect condition, with the body corresponding to the perfection of the Head since it is bound together.

There are a few interesting factors to examine when considering the last two phrases of this verse. The Old Testament background of the term *perfect* indicates a filling, which flows from the higher or greater and benefits the lower or lesser (i.e. from God to man, to the lands, to the Temple, to the living creatures). It never flows in the other direction.

There is only one faith and knowledge that is desirable; that is the faith and knowledge of God's Son. No man is perfect as He is. There is no standard of perfection in manhood except the Messiah and Him alone.

The filling that takes place is not only quantitative, but personal and qualitative.

The Apostle says that Christ and the church make up one body. Therefore, we are to think of ourselves in this way. Christ is the Head, we are the members of the body. According to the Bible, the essence of perfection is determined by being in the right relationship to God, who is clean, holy, and perfect.

Scripture reveals that there are two statuses available to man or to individuals: you are either *in Christ* or outside Christ; you either have a right relationship with God, or you do not. You are not a little perfect or increasingly perfect. There is no in- between. You are either pregnant, or you are not.

Christ is perfect, and He makes the members of His body perfect. *Amen!*

16

The Perfect Man

> *Till we all come in* (into) *the unity of the faith, and of the knowledge of the Son of God, unto a perfect* (mature) *man, unto the measure of the stature of the fullness of Christ* [Eph. 4:13].

In Hebrew, the term *making perfect* is synonymous with "sanctifying." What is the meaning of *making perfect* in the verse *Till we all come in* (into) *the unity of the faith, unto a perfect* (mature) *man, unto the measure of the stature of the fullness of Christ* [Eph. 4:13]?

In this verse, the Hebrew meaning of *perfect* prevails. It means that the reality is to be fulfilled when a certain man is found, not when an ideal is discovered. Further, the perfection is achieved because the death of the appointed One has the essence of a sacrifice, and the ministry is fulfilled.

The church is basically moving forward and coming closer to Christ, but that does not mean she is gradually improving. The church is and remains imperfect. However, one day her hope and joy will be fulfilled. Then she will realize that the Messiah is the One . . . *who of God is made unto us wisdom, and righteousness, and sanctification, and redemption* [1 Cor. 1:30].

"What is the highest perfection of Christians? Full manhood is in Christ," according to John Calvin, who realizes it is our responsibility to mature in Christ and that we are to strive to do so.

People can be divided into two categories: the foolish ones who do not seek growth *in Christ*, and those who do. The person who is *in Christ* is perfect in all respects because he or she is *in Christ*.

A question should be asked: What and who is meant by the term *a perfect man*? There are several alternatives to consider.

First, one group espouses the idea that it means each person is to mature and become a perfect individual. Then, there would be in time a community composed of mature saints who have achieved perfection.

Consequently, Christ's role as the standard of manhood and the object of one's faith and knowledge would be altered or compromised. This alternative places the emphasis on personal growth as the result of personal effort. This approach has met strong opposition because it is not an acceptable interpretation.

Second, there is the idea that the whole church is growing rather than the individual saints or members. Paul's letter reveals that the whole body of Christ is growing, not just the individual members.

The perfection, as stated in Ephesians, may well be the result of how and where the elect walk together in unity. The objective of their walk together can be attained only as members of Christ's body.

Therefore, the objective toward which the body is moving is a perfect church. This perfection does not exclude the individual members, even though it moves as an entity. Even though the church is progressing towards perfection, it realizes that Christ is greater than the church.

Third, Christ remains not only the head of the body, but retains His position and authority as the ruler of the body and as the source of its life. This approach does not emphasize an important happening: at the end of this journey they are going to meet the Lord Jesus Christ.

Unfortunately, these people replace the miracle of expecting to meet the Lord Jesus Christ with such things as the process and progress of pious convictions; incorporating or elevating sacraments or rites; and activities in the church no matter what they may be, plus growth of numbers. What a contrast!

Fourth, the language in this verse suggests that the perfect man is none other than the Lord Jesus Christ Himself.

The Church is a procession of people marching forward, who are well-equipped, who endure hardships, who are brave and joyful, and who look forward with eager anticipation to meeting the triumphant Lord.

According to the Synoptic Gospels, Paul's letters, Hebrews, and the Book of Revelation, the actual moment of meeting Him is the day of His second coming. Therefore, it is well to recognize that the word *perfect* is accepted by some to mean the last state in a progression.

In the Greek Old Testament the word *tamin* is used several times. It means "whole," "sound," "true," or "complete." In the New Testament the Greek word *teleiōs* is used. It means "ended, full-grown, fully developed," and "complete."

In addition, it means to be turned with our whole will and being toward God, just as He is turned toward us. This turning is an obedient response and an effort carried out in faith. It is the result of the Spirit working within us; it is not a situation whereby we are improving a moral condition by exerting more effort to improve our conduct.

There is nothing in the Bible that speaks of perfection as being the end result of an ever-increasing goodness or conduct residing in an individual, or group, or community.

Christ's command to *Be ye . . . perfect* [Matt. 5:48] can bring forth only one response, and that is faith. How do we examine and accept this truth?

Our obedience in faith is not the beginning of a journey whereby we progress in some vague way or manner to ever higher moral plateaus. No! It is not! It is the acceptance of grace, God's grace, which is always whole, sound, true, and complete. Our lives are to be lived in response to this encounter.

Perfect is something that belongs to God, and the only way we receive it is as a gift. It cannot be earned. It can only be received as a result of coming into contact with God.

Everything that God has and is is perfect. It is never less than 100 percent. It is never partial nor unfulfilled. Our relationship to Him determines the portion of our share in His wholeness and completeness. The portion is there. The question is: What do we do? Do we partake of it, or do we ignore or reject it?

Paul in his first letter to the Corinthians describes spiritual gifts and the diversity contained in them. He describes the diversity of the members of a human body, saying, *For the body is not one member, but many* [1 Cor. 12:14]. This passage should enlighten us and enable us to better understand the teachings of Christ as presented by Paul. The Apostle urges the followers to pool their gifts, to bind themselves together, and in so doing to benefit each other. The different gifts were given by God not for the individual to enhance himself or herself, but to help and to share with the other members of the body, which is Christ.

Remember, it has been said before, but it bears repeating: different members of the body, different functions to perform, yet joined in such a way as to form a unity.

We are to be concerned about our union with each other even though we have different gifts. The different gifts all come from the same giver, so where then is thy boasting?

The phrase *so also is Christ* is to be interpreted. The comparison in this verse is to us, members of the body of Christ, not to the Lord Jesus Himself.

This is important and should be recognized as such: Christ honors us, He wants us to be discerning, and recognized as members of His body. Christ is the Head and we are members, individually and collectively, of His particular body.

The Apostle concludes the thirteenth verse with the words *unto the measure of the stature of the fullness of Christ* [Eph. 4:13]. What does this mean?

Thoughts generated by this phrase are "age," "height," "length," "capacity," and "greatness." All of these terms are important in this instance.

The Apostle wants to convey the image of a person progressing from adolescence to adulthood. He wants us to see how this perfection is going to be attained. The *perfect man* is not only the Head Himself, Jesus Christ, but also the body and those who are part of it. That body, that man, that church will be perfect when every single part and portion is perfect.

This does not mean that each part will be equal and identical in every respect. The toe is different from the finger, the foot from the hand, the arm from the leg, and so on. The various parts are different, they have different functions to perform, and they have different capabilities.

There is no suggestion in the New Testament of sameness, or that all the members are to conform to a certain platform. Remember, counterfeits are always mechanical and identical in most respects. The glory of the body of Christ, or church, is the extraordinary variety and variation, yet unity is achieved by dissimilar parts.

What really matters in the church is not the particular calling, or office, or the specific grace given *according to the measure of the gift of Christ* [Eph. 4:7]. But it does matter that each one is sound, true, complete, and whole in his or her position.

If a cup, glass, or jar is full to overflowing then you can say each one is full even though they contain differing amounts. That the amounts are different is not critical. What is important? That each one enjoys and rejoices in the fullness received.

When the church, or body, is complete, when the *perfect man* will have arrived and all the saints will have been gathered in, then the whole body will be proportionately full and complete. It will be perfect.

There is a sense in which Christ's fullness is not complete without us. This is seen in His self-abnegation and self-humiliation. He has subjected Himself to this although He is the Head of the church, His body. He has joined Himself to the body of which we are part.

Therefore, He is not complete without us, because His body is not complete until we all share in His fullness and are made perfect. Then His fullness is in every one of us.

The analogy of the body as well as the whole structure and nature of it helps us understand this truth. The life is in the blood that goes to every part of the body, and the fullness of the head is in the toes and fingers as well is in the other parts.

It is our failure to realize and accept this that leads to problems in the local congregations and the church at large. The pastors and teachers have to appeal to and urge people to attend church or class and to participate by accepting various responsibilities.

One major factor contributing to this deplorable situation is that people do not see themselves as members of Christ's body. They think if the pastor or teacher is a member of the body, and if they are on good terms with that individual, then they will be in a right relationship with God and Christ.

They think they are honoring the church by attending or contributing spasmodically. They do not realize they are to strive to make up His fullness and to be in a right relationship with God. They are to grow *unto an holy temple in the Lord* [Eph. 2:21], they are to grow in grace, and they are to *come in* (into) *the unity of the faith, and of the knowledge of the Son of God* [Eph. 4:13].

We have a responsibility to meditate upon this *perfect* (mature) *man* that is *coming* and *unto the measure of the stature of the fullness of Christ* [Eph. 4:13].

We are not to concentrate upon our place or position in the church, because everyone is important. When we emphasize one over the other we tend to go wrong. Also, we tend to go wrong when we overstress the differences or distinctions between the laity and clergy.

It is all right to emphasize certain offices, but we must not detract from others. Every member of the body, every office in the church is important.

The goal is not the office or position, it is

> *Till we all come in* (into) *the unity of the faith, and of the knowledge of the Son of God, . . . unto the measure of the stature of the fullness of Christ* [Eph. 4:13].

Amen!

17

Henceforth

> *That we henceforth be no more children, tossed to and fro, and carried about with every wind of doctrine, by the sleight* (trickery) *of men, and cunning craftiness, whereby they lie in wait to deceive* [Eph. 4:14].

The fourteenth, fifteenth, and sixteenth verses contain important truths requiring scrutiny. They are the culmination of what we have been examining. Christ has given, by His grace, certain gifts that some be apostles, prophets, evangelists, pastors and teachers. These gifts were given for specific purposes.

> *For the perfecting* (equipping) *of the saints, for the work of the ministry, for edifying the body of Christ:* (and)
> *Till we all come in* (into) *the unity of the faith, and . . . knowledge of the Son of God, unto a perfect* (mature) *man, unto the measure of the stature of the fullness of Christ* [Eph. 4:12–13].

We are to reach this status for the benefit of Christ's body, the church. Please note, Paul says *children* in this fourteenth verse. He is speaking of all the members. He does not say "child." He is addressing all the members as an entity. This is a case of adjusting the mindset and realizing Paul is writing to us collectively. He is writing to the members of the body of Christ.

Scripture must be taken in its context. Paul has been talking about the future and what will happen when we reach maturity in faith as members of Christ's body. Then he says, *That we henceforth be*. He inserts this phrase in order to emphasize the contrast between what we are and what we shall be. He wants us to continue focusing on the ultimate goal.

Paul was endowed with many gifts. One of these was profound wisdom as a teacher. He had the ability to deal with people as they were and to satisfy their knowledge or lack of it. He exhibits this ability by inserting the word *henceforth*.

He reminds the Ephesians that there are certain things they should realize, even if they are negative. We must be aware of the negatives in order to achieve a positive position. One reason for the present state of the church is that we do not know certain negatives.

The first thing to understand in examining this fourteenth verse is that we all begin our Christian life, or life *in Christ*, as children. This is true whether we begin this life at the age of eight or eighty. This should be obvious, but it is not. Paul is doing certain things at this point by saying, *That we henceforth be no more children.*

"Those are children who have not yet taken a step in the way of the Lord, but still hesitate, who have not yet determined what road they ought to choose, but move sometimes in one direction and sometimes in another, always doubtful, always wavering. But those are thoroughly founded in the doctrine of Christ who, although not yet perfect, have so much wisdom and vigour as to choose what is best, and proceed steadily in the right course. Thus the life of believers, longing constantly for their appointed state, is like adolescence . . . . as if they were in progress beyond childhood. After being born in Christ, we ought to grow, so as not to be children in understanding," according to John Calvin.

He reminds us that our life *in Christ* is a new life. It is not a continuation or addendum to any other life. Our knowledge and expertise in other areas are not transferable. They do not enable us to assume the mantle of mature Christians.

The designation *children* draws a distinct line between the person *in Christ* and the one who is not. What is required? How does it happen? Consider the encounter between Jesus and Nicodemus when the latter asked, *How can a man be born when he is old* [John 3:4]? Jesus responds by telling Nicodemus something very simple and straightforward, . . . *Ye must be born again* [John 3:7]. He actually said, *Marvel not that I said unto thee, Ye must be born again* [John 3:7].

Think of that! You must go back to the beginning; *you must learn to think anew—to think as a child—to ask questions as a child—to be inquisitive as a child—and to desire knowledge as a child!*

"This statement implies the whole principle of growth and development. We are to start as children, and from that point we are to grow, develop, and mature," according to Martyn Lloyd-Jones.

Nicodemus thought a new life would be incredible. Christ tried to teach him that even in his bodily life, the marvelous power of God is hidden. Calvin provides additional insight, saying, "If in this frail and transitory life God acts so powerfully. . . how absurd it is to want to measure by the apprehension of our own mind His secret work in the heavenly and supernatural life and believe no more than we can see!"

When Christ tells Nicodemus not to marvel, He means that we should not shake our heads in disbelief and as a result impede our faith, but we should admire the work of God. We should never doubt for a moment that by the power of God and the workings of the Holy Spirit we are refashioned and made new. However, the way God does this is not revealed to us. Peter says, *As newborn babes, desire the sincere* (pure) *milk of the word, that ye may grow thereby* [1 Pet. 2:2].

The New Testament places a special emphasis on little children and the different stages of life. However, despite this emphasis there is a tendency on our part to either ignore it or to forget it. I doubt that you have ever heard one or two sermons on this important truth. There is a tendency by most people to think that once they have become a member of a church, or made a profession of faith, or attend church services regularly that they have arrived at the pinnacle of the Christian life.

Conversion or a profession of faith is not an end but a beginning. During World War II right after the allies had been victorious in Africa, someone asked Churchill if it was the beginning of the end. He responded, only as he would, by saying "No, but it was the end of the beginning."

When becoming members of Christ's body, everyone should think of their life *in Christ* in the same way. It is only "the end of the beginning." There is much, much more to follow.

We must eliminate the idea that becoming a Christian or a member of Christ's body is the end of the story. If we do not, we will miss much of what is available. Further, we will be confused about the teachings contained in the New Testament.

The Apostle's letters to Timothy and Titus describe what the novices should not do and should not be asked to do. We are to know about those truths. Unfortunately, the teaching today is to give the babes, the novices, the converts something to do. Elect them to office, place them in positions of authority, get them involved in responsible areas.

However, the teaching of the New Testament Epistles is for the babe, novice, or recent convert to become fit, qualified, and knowledgeable, to give, and to learn to be of service to the Lord.

The New Testament is rather clear on another point. Everyone who becomes a member of Christ's body does so as a babe or a novice. He or she may have many attributes in his or her field, but as new members of the fellowship, they are babes. Failure to realize this has been detrimental to the body of Christ, the church, and local congregations.

Each person starts as a child, then develops and grows. What is required of a person? Not natural ability, not secular positions or power. What is required is spiritual understanding, spiritual apprehension, and spiritual knowledge of the truth.

Paul says we ought not to be like children. He says those who are still children have not walked in the way of the Lord: They hesitate, they go one way, then another, they have doubts, they waver, and they are misled.

However, those grounded in Christ's teachings, although not yet perfect, have much wisdom and vigor, enabling them to proceed on the right course.

Children have certain characteristics and inclinations. However, after being born *in Christ* we should grow, we should not remain children in our faith and understanding. It is essential to grow *in Christ*. If we do not we shall remain children. We shall end as we began.

There is a most important truth that cannot be ignored or overlooked: we are to appropriate and grasp what has been made possible, and what has been promised to us. We are to . . . *grow in grace, and in the knowledge of our Lord and Saviour Jesus Christ* [2 Pet. 3:18].

Paul describes the children with two interesting metaphors, *tossed to and fro* and *carried about*. These phrases describe the characteristics of children. One of those characteristics is the instability of children.

This phrase does not mean tossed about by waves, but that we are like waves, *tossed to and fro* and constantly in motion. That we do not rest firmly on anything substantial or of substance, like the Word of God. The Greek word for "tossed" is *kludonizom*, which means "agitated." The same meaning is found in James when he says, *But let him ask in faith, nothing wavering* (not doubting). *For he that wavereth* (doubts) *is like a wave of the sea driven with the wind and tossed* [Jas. 1:6]. Even though a different Greek word for "tossed," *Rhipizomal*, is used, it also means "agitated."

John Calvin, in his inimitable fashion, provides additional insight regarding Paul's statement . . . "*tossed to and fro, and carried about (with every wind of doctrine)*. In two elegant metaphors he illustrates the wretched hesitation of those who do not rest firmly on the Word of the Lord. The first is taken from small ships . . . Then, he compares them with straws . . . , which are carried hither and thither . . . , and often in opposite directions. So, . . . must these unsteady people be moved whose basis is not God's eternal truth. This the just punishment against all who look to men rather than to God. Paul declares . . . that faith, which rests on the Word of God, stands unshaken against all the attacks of Satan."

There is nothing so characteristic of the sea as its restlessness, its constant motion and change. This is also true of children.

Paul compares the children with other things that are carried hither and yon by the waves and the wind, often times in opposite directions.

Another characteristic is the fickleness of children. We are all aware how rapidly a child can change—from having a happy smile to exhibiting a mournful cry. Actually, the child cannot help it, because he or she is a child. But, this also happens with adults.

The lack of self-control is another characteristic of children. One reason for this is that they are accustomed to their parents or adults controlling them. Have not we always been relieved to hear that our children or grandchildren are "street saints" when we know them as "house devils"?

Children are creatures of impulses and moods. They know little about self-discipline and have great difficulty in controlling themselves. Self-control is a difficult task. A child does not control himself or herself, but is more than capable of expressing himself or herself.

When we are babes, or children *in Christ*, we have the ability to express ourselves, but when we mature we have the ability to think about what Christ wants and what the Word of God is saying to us. That is a significant difference.

The child wants something and wants it at once. The mature person leaves it to the will of God and knows, as Abraham did, that God will act according to His plan and timetable.

John Calvin states with assurance and calmness, "Paul declares that faith which rests upon the Word of God stands unshaken against all the attacks of Satan."

Children also tend to react excessively or violently when displeased. A child either likes or dislikes something, and that feeling or expression can change from one minute to the next. Usually there is no in between, no middle ground.

What does Scripture say? *For God hath not given us the spirit of fear; but of power, and of love, and of a sound mind* [2 Tim. 1:7]. In this verse, sound mind means discipline and self-control.

To have this capability in the right sense and way, we must be endued from on high. It is God who equips us with this power, this capability. A child holds its views stubbornly, yet at the same time changes from one extreme point of view to another. You never know when their opinions or viewpoints will change or how dramatically.

Therefore, at times, we see a child or childlike person in a state of perpetual turmoil or mental agitation. These traits may be true of the adults who have recently become Christians, or members of the body of Christ, and have not matured in the faith.

We have all experienced situations where children become upset or troubled by something, so they get together, support each others' woes, and continue to stir the pot of agitation. They feel the world is about to end, and that they must take some action. They are like the waves of the sea: *tossed to and fro.*

In summary, we can describe the child in light of the following: instability, fickleness, constant motion and agitation, lack of discipline and self-control, the inability to control negative reactions, and stubbornness.

The child's life is lived on the surface. He or she has not developed inner reserves on which to rely or to fall back upon. Please do not misunderstand. What has been said is a description, not a criticism of a child. It is not something the child can help. But as the child grows, develops, and matures these childlike traits are discarded, hopefully.

Therefore, the Apostle says, *That we henceforth be no more children.*

Another factor about a child is his ability to be misled and to be deceived. The Apostle says, *carried about with every wind of doctrine.*

The Apostle by this beautiful metaphor is referring to all the doctrines of man. God has given us His Word so that we will remain unmoved. But men lead us astray by the inventions or craftiness of their minds.

Calvin continues to expound upon Paul's statement "*. . . with every wind of doctrine*. In a beautiful metaphor he calls all the doctrines of men, by which we are drawn away from the simplicity of the Gospel, 'winds'. God gave us His Word, in which when we have struck root we stay uninvolved; but men lead us astray in all directions by their inventions.

"When he adds, *By the cunning of men*, he means that there will always be imposters, who menace and attack our faith; but, if we are armed with the truth of God, they will fail. . . . But Satan can never rest without striving to darken by his lies the pure doctrine of Christ, and God wants to try our faith with these struggles. . . . But we who have embraced the law, the prophets, and the Gospel, let us not doubt that we shall receive the fruit which Paul declares—that all the impostures of men will not harm us. We must . . . seek for sound doctrine from the church, for God has committed it to her charge."

There is an interesting dichotomy to consider at this point: Satan can never rest and is always striving to darken or tarnish the pure doctrine of Christ, yet God wants our faith to be tried and tested by these very struggles. We are to know and to rely upon the teachings of Christ. If we do not know them, how can we use them?

This metaphor describes the reality of the wind. It comes from one direction and before you know it, it changes its course. Similarly, a child can be carried in every conceivable direction by diverse types of teaching.

A child tends to believe everything he or she is told. Therefore, it is easy prey to any imposter that comes along. Paul warned the Ephesian elders, saying,

> *For I know this, that after my departing shall grievous* (savage) *wolves enter in among you, not sparing the flock* [Acts 20:29].
>
> *Therefore watch, and remember, . . . I ceased not to warn every one night and day with tears.*
> *. . . I commend you to God, and to the word of his grace, which is able to build you up, and to give you an inheritance among all them which are sanctified* [Acts 20:31–32].

It is interesting that Paul said these things to the elders at Ephesus. Why? Because he was concerned about them.

An important question: why is it relatively easy to impose upon a child? Because of his ignorance, his lack of knowledge, and because the child has not had the time, the ability, or the understanding to develop a foundation and the standards for making judgments.

How can the child tell the difference between that which is right and that which is wrong? By acquiring the proper knowledge. It is unfortunate when a child does not acquire the right knowledge, but it is even more so when an adult does not pursue knowledge and gain it.

It can be said of a child that it dislikes being taught and submitting to discipline. A child is impatient and does not like being taught slowly. He or she wants to advance rapidly. How many times have we seen a child when being shown how to do something say, "I'll do it myself" or "Give it to me, I know how to do it"?

The child basically rejects the idea that it takes time to grow and develop from one stage to another. He or she dislikes learning and practicing the scales in music. They want to play like accomplished musicians.

Time, discipline, and learning are required to develop as a member of Christ's body.

Another characteristic of the child is that it likes novelty, change, something new and different.

What happens when a child is playing with one of its favorite toys, and suddenly it receives a new one that appeals to the eye? The favorite one is discarded for the new one. The childish mind likes change and craves for something new.

You may recall that the people in Athens were described as spending *... their time in nothing else, but either to tell, or to hear some new thing* [Acts 17:21]. How this statement applies today! Especially to the many church members who pursue or are subject to change and newness.

Further, the child likes entertainment and excitement, especially when it is accompanied by what it terms freedom. How many children have a favorite aunt, uncle, or friend of the family who removes the restraint of discipline and indulges every whim of the child?

These characteristics describing a child are also true of the individuals growing and developing as members of the body of Christ. They are *tossed to and fro* and are *carried about*. They dislike studying and submitting to the discipline required to learn. They say, "Why do I have to read or study that?" They like novelty and change, something new and different. They like entertainment and excitement; and freedom from control and discipline. The Apostle wanted to impress these truths on the Ephesians (and us), because if they did not recognize them and understand them, then they would not grow and develop as members of Christ's body.

Another childish trait is the susceptibility to showmanship. The child is not able to dissect or to assess the real content behind the facade of the showman, and lacking the necessary knowledge, insight, and understanding, he or she can be mislead.

The self-confident manner of the showman appeals to a child. That is why he or she has to be protected, disciplined, and taught.

The Apostle Paul's teaching is important. He wants us to reject the *sleight* (trickery) *of men* and their *cunning craftiness*. This requires three things: The child in the faith must realize he or she is a child; the child must realize because he or she is a child that it is in a dangerous or tenuous position; and the child must realize it needs to learn.

May God grant us the ability to put away childish things. May He grant us discipline, knowledge, and understanding. May He grant us a desire for His truth and the diligence to pursue it. When He does grant these petitions, may we realize our responsibilities in serving the Lord. Therefore,

- may we not be *tossed to and fro*;
- may we not be *carried about with every wind of doctrine*;
- may the Holy Spirit illuminate the Word in our hearts and minds;
- may we embrace the Gospel; and
- may we seek sound doctrine as presented in the teachings of our Lord Jesus Christ.

Amen!

18

Cunning Craftiness

> *That we henceforth be no more children, tossed to and fro, and carried about with every wind of doctrine, by the sleight* (trickery) *of men, and cunning craftiness, whereby they lie in wait to deceive* [Eph. 4:14].

Why is it that we like to hear the nice things, the good thoughts, the pleasant ideas and comments? Why do we like to hear certain passages from Scripture: *In the beginning*; *God is love*, the Twenty-third Psalm, John 3:16, John 17, and many others? Have you ever wondered about this? There are many beautiful thoughts expressed in Scripture, and certainly they warm our hearts and minds.

The ideas conveyed by love, joy, and peace rank extremely high with most people. There is usually great interest in the words light, truth, and compassion. And of course in the modern vernacular there is the oft-heard statement, "tell it like it is." However, that applies to the teller not to the "tellee."

There is less interest in hearing about obeying commandments, doing the will of our Father who is in heaven, learning, and acquiring knowledge. There is even less interest when it comes to warnings, rebukes, and chastisements, since those things turn us off.

Then there is the ultimate factor that can grab and shake us: The realization that we have been going in the wrong direction, and that our mindset must change.

Think for a moment of Paul. This brilliant, well-educated person changed 180 degrees. He was going one way, he was self-satisfied, he knew that he was right, and what happened? He encountered the Lord Jesus Christ on the road to Damascus. It was one of the most momentous events in history and changed its course almost as much as it changed Paul. He started his journey

> AND Saul yet breathing out threatenings and slaughter (murder) against the disciples of the Lord [Acts 9:1].
>
> ... he came near Damascus: and suddenly there shined round about him a light from heaven:
> ... and (he) heard a voice saying unto him, Saul, Saul, why persecutest thou me [Acts 9:3–4]?

The response by Paul is amazing and revealing. He did not lose his composure, but had the presence of mind to utter the words,

> ... Who art thou, Lord? And the Lord said, I am Jesus whom thou persecutest: ...
> And he trembling and astonished said, Lord, what wilt thou have me to do [Acts 9:5–6]?

We may never have an experience similar to Paul's. However, we do have the scriptures, preaching and teaching, that still small voice which speaks to us, and the Holy Spirit to reveal God's will for us and to be our Comforter. Like Paul, we are to listen for God to speak to us, and we are to ask the same question he did, ... *Lord, what wilt thou have me to do* [Acts 9:6]?

Note the change in Paul when he was confronted by the Lord Jesus Christ, when he accepted Him, and when he obeyed His commands.

Paul learned the truth about Christ. He learned the good, the wonderful, and the beautiful. He also learned to accept with a grateful heart and humility the warnings, rebukings, corrections, and hard teachings of the Master. He delved, he sought, he searched, he asked, and he questioned. He loved every part of Christ's teachings and commandments.

What happened to Paul is supposed to happen and should happen to each of us. He changed from focusing on his own capabilities and ideas to focusing on Jesus Christ. He put the Master first.

What does this have to do with the phrase, *That we henceforth be no more children*? Children in the faith, or in any field, must receive encouragement, but they must also receive instruction in both the positive and negative facets and nuances in their field of endeavor.

Paul specifically stated, *That we henceforth be no more children, tossed to and fro*. If we note the words and meaning, he issued a very clear warning. We are not to be carried about by *every wind of doctrine*;

the sleight (trickery) *of men; cunning craftiness; and* (those who) *lie in wait to deceive.*

What warnings did our Lord Jesus Christ issue? He said,

> *Beware of false prophets, which come to you in sheep's clothing, but inwardly they are ravening* (ravenous) *wolves* [Matt. 7:15].

Unfortunately, for the most part the members of the organized church do not like to hear the warnings, the rebukings, and the commandments. They ignore them. Yet Paul said to the Ephesian elders,

> *Take heed . . . unto yourselves, . . . to feed* (shepherd) *the church of God, which he hath purchased with his own blood.*
> *For I know this, that after my departing shall grievous* (savage) *wolves, enter in among you, not sparing the flock* [Acts 20:28–29].
>
> *Therefore watch, and remember, . . . I ceased not to warn every one night and day with tears* [Acts 20:31].

The New Testament Epistles contain arguments, disputations, reasons, and warnings concerning our thoughts and activities. Paul told the Philippians,

> *Beware of dogs, beware of evil workers, beware of the concision* (mutilation) [Phil. 3:2].

We are not to curtail our teaching, preaching, and learning, nor are we to omit the warnings and rebukings. Paul says,

> *Beware lest any man spoil* (plunder) *you through philosophy and vain* (empty) *deceit, after* (according to) *the tradition of men, after the rudiments of the world, and not after* (the basic principles of) *Christ* [Col. 2:8].

In addition, it should be noted that warnings against false teachers are contained in: 1 Peter, Jude, 1 John, and the Book of Revelation.

It can be safely stated that the New Testament warns the members of Christ's body to beware of the terrible, ever-present danger of being led astray by false teachings. Implicit in this teaching is the fact that we are to become knowledgeable, grow in the faith, and acquire understanding.

It is interesting to note the strong language used in the New Testament with respect to warnings and dangers:

> *Woe unto you, scribes and Pharisees, hypocrites* [Matt. 23:23].

> *(For many walk, of whom I have told you often, . . . that they are the enemies of the cross of Christ* [Phil. 3:18].
>
> . . . *because they received not the love of the truth, that they might be saved.*
> *And for this cause God shall send them strong delusion, . . .*
> *That they all might be damned* (condemned) *who believed not the truth, but had pleasure in unrighteousness* [2 Thess. 2:10–12].

There is strong language in the New Testament in addition to what we have considered: John writes about the "anti-Christ." Peter refers to *damnable heresies* and *pernicious ways* saying,

> *BUT there were false prophets also among the people, even as there shall be false teachers among you, who privily* (secretly) *shall bring in damnable* (destructive) *heresies, even denying the Lord that bought them, and bring upon themselves swift destruction.*
> *And many shall follow their pernicious* (deceptive) *ways; by reason of whom the way of truth shall be evil* (blasphemed) *spoken of* [2 Pet. 2:1–2].

False teachings are the result of the serpent working. Subtlety, innuendos, and deceit are characteristic of the life of man. It was for this reason that the Lord Jesus Christ called and provided apostles, prophets, evangelists, pastors, and teachers.

Some people have criticized Paul. They have said he was narrow and intolerant, and did not want anyone to disagree with his teaching. However, we have quoted from our Lord Jesus as well as from Peter and John. They all agree and support the teachings of our Lord and Master.

Paul's words in the verse being considered are an excellent description of the current status of the body of Christ. The members of the body must be aware of these things. If we are, then we must understand what Paul is teaching and what he means.

First Paul emphasizes *every wind of doctrine*. Paul in this beautiful metaphor identifies all the doctrines of men, which blow as the wind and drive people away from the Gospel of Christ.

He is informing them that God's Word and His teachings keep us unmoved and on the right course. However, the inventions and interpretations of men lead us astray.

Paul wants us aware of the fact that, literally, we are surrounded by evil, false teachings, and heresies. Lest we think this unusual, we should remember that this was true following the life, death, and resurrection of our Lord Jesus Christ.

Next the Apostle says, *by the sleight* (trickery) *of men, and cunning craftiness, whereby they lie in wait to deceive.* The word *sleight* is very interesting. It is only used this one time in Scripture. It means "playing at dice" and "to cheat."

Paul wants us aware of the fact that there is always the opportunity for deceit, trickery, cheating, and chicanery. He wants us to know that while you are not watching carefully the person throwing the dice can manipulate them and achieve the result he desires.

The Apostle wants the members of the body of Christ cognizant of false teachers, their teachings, and how they can mislead them if they are not knowledgeable.

The Apostle goes on to say that they do this by their *cunning craftiness*. This calls attention to the trickery, cleverness, and subtlety of their teachings and methods. They know what they are doing and proceed to do it.

These words reveal that there are imposters who will successfully attack our faith unless we are armed with God's truth.

"Satan can never rest without striving to darken by his lies the pure doctrine of Christ, and God wants to try our faith with these struggles," according to John Calvin as he warns us against this insidious foe, who plagues us day in and day out. The best and strongest remedy against these attacks is to bring forth the doctrine we learn from Christ and His apostles.

There is the ongoing battle between those accepting the teachings of God and those succumbing to the teachings of men and becoming subservient to their authority. Some teach that if you are in doubt it is in vain to consult the word of God, but that you must abide by the decrees of men.

However, we should remember the Apostle Paul declares that if we embrace the law, the prophets, and the Gospel we shall not succumb to false teachings and the fraudulent claims of men. Even though they may attack us, they will not prevail.

We are to seek sound doctrine and teachings from Scripture and from the members of the body of Christ.

The Apostle says in the fourteenth verse, *whereby they lie in wait.* What does this mean? The original interpretation is to follow someone and "to track him as a wild animal tracks and follows its prey." Think of predators that track and follow their prey.

The Apostle uses this description to emphasize a certain truth. We are confronted by something that is very methodical and planned almost to perfection. By this phrase, the Apostle teaches that *the sleight of men* lies in wait to deceive. Further, *the sleight of men and cunning craftiness* operate on the basis of trying to capture or entrap individuals. The members of Christ's body are to be aware of this.

A question to consider: Are we aware of these things at this time? Do we realize that error is not only a negative, but that it may be very active and positive? We are to realize that error is not just the absence of the full truth or a complete teaching, but it is a positive evil.

This point is stressed because some say that sin is merely the absence of good qualities. Further, there is a sentimental teaching that we should not say a person is really bad, but should say that the person is not really good.

This teaching continues by saying that there is no such thing as a positive evil, or a positively evil teaching. It denies the teaching of Scripture, which emphasizes the evil character of false teachings.

A second characteristic of false teaching is that it is planned and organized, that it does not happen accidentally.

Missionaries report that they encounter more difficulties with false teachings, religions, and errors than they do with unbelief. After the missionary has received some converts, they become prey for evil and false teachings.

How often it happens that recent converts of any age, or those who are led back into the fold, become prey for evil and false teachings. They become the targets for creating doubts in their minds as to the authority of Scripture, the person of our Lord Jesus Christ, and other essential teachings regarding being members of the body of Christ. Their ignorance can lead them astray temporarily or permanently.

I remember when I first started teaching years ago, our minister said to me, "Bob, you have begun to teach the high school students, and I want to tell you something: you have to beware of false teachings. Now that you are teaching you will find that some people will want to influence you and to supply you with materials and books that are not based on the authority of the Bible or that do not open Scripture to you. So beware of the material you use."

False teachers have certain characteristics: they lie in wait, they are well-organized, they have extraordinary zeal, they have financial resources, they make sacrifices, they have literature, they conduct meetings, and they are willing to work.

The false teachers "lie in wait." They make their plans, and they execute them. This has happened since the garden of Eden and the Fall of man. Look how Adam and Eve were approached and how they both succumbed.

A third characteristic of false teaching is its subtlety. Look at the words Paul uses in this fourteenth verse, *cunning craftiness, sleight* (trickery) *of men,* and *lie in wait to deceive.* These words not only describe the attractiveness of it, but they inform us as to why it attracts individuals, especially those who are children in the faith.

The false teaching tells us that we do not need to spend much time studying Paul's letter to the Ephesians, and that we do not have to struggle to understand Christ's teachings and doctrine.

They want to say the truth is so simple all you have to do is simply believe, do some works, contribute some money, and you will have everything. It is all so simple. It offers shortcuts that will produce immediate and direct results. No effort is required. They emphasize that it is either easy, or else someone else will do it for you. However, that is not what Scripture teaches.

How can we recognize the subtlety or trickery of false teachings? It is anything that detracts or takes away from the Lord Jesus Christ. This does not mean they deny Him or ignore Him directly, but obliquely seek to detract from Him or diminish His stature.

It means that they emphasize other factors or entities such as a priest, minister, pope, General Assembly, church, the Virgin Mary, dead saints, or whatever. Any one of these approaches detracts from the Lord and exalts a person, a collection of people, an institution, or an organization.

It is no longer Christ alone and Christ exclusively. "Everything is to be tested by the position given to the Lord Jesus Christ because He is central, He is unique, He is above and beyond all, and He is the pinnacle. All others are below. If this is not the teaching, then it is false," to quote and paraphrase Lloyd-Jones.

What is to be our attitude with respect to false teaching? *It is to be rejected, hated, and opposed.* We have seen how our Lord and His apostles opposed it and warned the people against it.

Do we subscribe to current teachings which ignore or dislike warnings, and criticize false teachings? Do we agree with those who say that a spirit of love is not compatible with denouncing negative, critical, and blatant errors?

The very simple answer is that our Lord denounced evil and false teachings. He called them *ravening wolves, whited sepulchers*, and *blind guides*. The Apostle Paul said, *Whose god is their belly, and whose glory is in their shame, who* (set their) *mind* (on) *earthly things* [Phil. 3:19]. That is New Testament language!

The church is in her current condition because we do not follow the New Testament teachings and their exhortations, but confine ourselves to the so-called positive and simple Gospel, which fails to stress the negatives and the criticisms. What is the result?

People do not recognize error when they encounter it. They accept what appears to be nice, easy, and simple. They become prey for the predatory beasts that track them and pounce on them with cleverness and subtlety.

It is not pleasant and enjoyable to be negative, to denounce and expose error, but it is our responsibility, our duty, as members of Christ's body to do so. This sentence of which the fourteenth verse is an integral part begins by saying, *And he* (himself) *gave some apostles; and some prophets; and some evangelists; and some, pastors and teachers* [Eph. 4:11]. Why did he give them? For the perfecting of the saints, for the work of the ministry, and for the edifying of the body of Christ. He gave them that we might know the positives as well as the negatives, and that we might grow *unto the measure of the stature of the fullness of Christ* [Eph. 4:13].

May God open our eyes and give us understanding *in Christ*. May we be able to resist the wiles of Satan. May we *henceforth be no more children, tossed to and fro*. May we believe, think, and act as members of Christ's body.

Amen!

19

Growing Up Into Christ

> *But speaking the truth in love, may grow up into him in all things, which is the head, even Christ* [Eph. 4:15].

Paul informed the Ephesians that they were no longer to be children, destitute of reason and judgment. Instead, they were to grow in the truth revealed by and through the Lord Jesus Christ.

This verse [Eph. 4:15], introduces again the positive teachings of the Apostle with respect to the ministry of the church. The objective is to bring us *unto a perfect* (mature) *man, unto the measure of the stature of the fullness of Christ* [Eph. 4:13]. If we are to achieve this objective, we must realize where we are in our spiritual development, that we are children in the faith and thereby subject to the traits of children.

The Apostle enjoins us to grow in the truth and in love. Although we have not arrived at a mature condition, we are to speak the truth in love, and we are to grow up into Him in all things.

In addition, the truth of God is to be so strong and firm within us that we shall be able to withstand the contrivances and assaults of the evil one, although we have not attained full and complete strength as members of Christ's body. We are to progress each and every day, and year by year.

Paul declares that the purpose of this progress is that Christ may have an exalted position, and for the Ephesians to grow up in Him. Christ is to increase, and all others are to decrease, in order that the church may grow. Our increase is to be in proportion to the Head, which is Christ.

The individual members are not to be self-centered, but they are to be diligent in searching for the truth as revealed in Christ Jesus. They are to be in harmony with the Head.

The fifteenth verse is interesting. It states, *But speaking the truth in love.*

First, we must understand the correct meaning of the word *speaking* in this verse.

The English word does not convey the accurate meaning of the word used by Paul. It means much more than just speaking. A more accurate translation would be "professing the truth," "knowing the truth," "walking in the truth," and "having or holding the truth in love." It encompasses our whole deportment. It means we are to be true, walk the truth in love, hold the truth, and grow into Christ in all things.

It is important to understand this verse and to consider it in its context. Also, consider Jesus' words in His high priestly prayer, *That they all may be one; as thou, Father, art in me, and I in thee, that they also may be one in us: that the world may believe that thou hast sent me* [John 17:21].

These verses are often abused and misquoted, especially by advocates of the Ecumenical Movement who propose a World Church and everyone becoming united under one banner. The verses are not to be taken out of context. As with all other verses in the Bible, they are to be taken in their context. We violate Scripture when we do not. When considering this fifteenth verse, keep in mind the Apostle's primary concern with this section of Scripture.

When he says *speaking the truth in love* he is not merely saying to be nice and loving. Unfortunately, today people want to attack this idea. They want to relate it to having fellowship with others, saying that that is of primary importance. We are told by those espousing this position that nothing is as important as having fellowship, and that unity in and of itself is of primary importance and the ultimate objective. Further, they suggest the lack of this type of unity is the main hindrance to evangelism and spreading the Gospel, and that revival cannot be realized without the unity of fellowship.

In addition, these people state that the reason the church is in its current condition is that so many people are outside the church. Further, the fact that there is division results from there not being unity among different groups or denominations.

They also say that nothing is as important as having one great church where fellowship and unity occupy the supreme positions. Since this is the case we are to tolerate anything and everything. As long as a person exhibits a nice, loving, friendly disposition, does good works, and contributes time or money, it is not important what they believe or do not believe.

That is not the teaching of Scripture. However, that is not important to them. They are more interested in their own ideas and those obtained from social and secular environments than from those contained in Scripture. Therefore, these people continue to espouse that:

- a person merely has to exhibit the "spirit of Christ," according to man's ideas or standards, not according to Scripture;
- an individual may be shaky or unsure about the Lordship of Christ; or
- one may not believe in the virgin birth, God incarnate, the atonement, or the resurrection.

They say that it is important for people to have an open mind; be tolerant of other opinions; be kind, friendly, and gracious; be concerned about others; be anxious to correct and make right all political and social wrongs; and to perform certain acts. These things are more important than learning and knowing the doctrinal views and teachings of Christ.

They also state that those who are outside the church have recently started attending services, attend infrequently, are not interested in doctrine, and do not accept all the teachings of Christ should be accepted into the fellowship of believers and have positions of influence. Further, certain doctrines and teachings of Scripture should not be strongly presented or defended lest you offend someone.

These are some of the ways in which people interpret the phrase *speaking the truth in love*.

This phrase has been interpreted as meaning you do not criticize and you do not strongly defend, because if you do then you are not exhibiting love. This phrase has come to mean that you praise everything and that there is a certain amount of truth in everything.

However, questions should be asked regarding these pronouncements: Is the above a correct interpretation of Paul's statement? What is really meant by *speaking the truth in love*?

The above-cited interpretations cannot be correct for a very simple reason: Paul does not admonish us to "speak lovingly." He says when you speak: profess the truth, hold the truth, and walk in the truth. This is not only what we are told to do; it is a command we are to obey. We are instructed to exhibit a loving spirit and our faith in Christ by *Speaking the truth in love* (that we) *may grow up into him in all things, which is the head, even Christ* [Eph. 4:15]. Once again, we are confronted with that old bugaboo: the secular mindset versus the teachings of Scripture.

The word *truth* in this verse is very interesting. It appears only twice in Scripture, here and in Galatians 4:16. The Greek word is *aletheuo,* and it means "to speak truly" or "to speak the truth." Therefore, this verse can be literally translated, "professing, holding, or walking the truth that I speak truly in love."

Since we have considered the words *speaking* and *truth* in this verse, we should also examine the word *love,* because Scripture says, *But speaking the truth in love.*

The Greek word for love in this verse is *agape.* What does it mean? It is used in the New Testament to describe God's attitude toward His Son when Jesus declared in His high priestly prayer,

> *And I have declared unto them thy name, and will declare it: that the love wherewith thou hast loved me may be in them, and I in them* [John 17:26].

Agape describes God's attitude toward man in these revealing words,

> *For God so loved the world, that he gave his only begotten Son, that whosoever believeth in him should not perish, but have everlasting life* [John 3:16].

> *But God commendeth* (demonstrates) *his* (own) *love toward us, in that, while we were yet sinners, Christ died for us* [Rom. 5:8].

And, *agape* describes His attitude toward those believing on the Lord Jesus Christ as revealed in the Master's own words saying,

> *He that hath my commandments, and keepeth them, he it is that loveth me: and he that loveth me shall be loved of my Father, and I will love him, and will manifest* (reveal) *myself to him* [John 14:21].

Agape is used to convey God's will to His children concerning their attitude toward one another.

> *A new commandment I give unto you, That ye love one another; as I have loved you* [John 13:34].

> *And the Lord make you to increase and abound in love one toward another, and toward all men, even as we do toward you.* [1 Thess. 3:12].

The Word is also used to express the essential nature of God.

> *He that loveth not knoweth not God; for God is love* [1 John 4:8].

God's nature is to love man. The Apostle John simply means "that God is the fountain of love. That this affection flows from God and is poured out where there is knowledge of Him. John is not speaking here of the essence of God, but is declaring what we experience Him to be," as respectfully and thankfully expressed by John Calvin.

Love in this context can be known only from the actions it prompts. God's love is seen in the gift of His Son.

God's love toward us is free. He freely loves us. Why? Because He loved us before we were born. This love is neither a love of complacency nor affection, nor is it because of any merit or excellency in those receiving it.

This love is an exercise in divine will, without any real cause except the true nature of God Himself.

> *But, God, who is rich in mercy, for his great love wherewith he loved us,* . . . [Eph. 2:4].

This love has its perfect expression among men in the Lord Jesus Christ.

> *And to know the love of Christ, which passeth knowledge, that ye might be filled with all the fullness of God* [Eph. 3:19].

> *And walk in love, as Christ also hath loved us, and hath given himself for us an offering and a sacrifice to God for a sweet-smelling savor* (aroma) [Eph. 5:2].

This love is the fruit of His Spirit in the members of Christ's body.

> *But the fruit of the Spirit is love, joy, peace, long-suffering, gentleness* (kindness), *goodness, faith* (faithfulness),
> *Meekness, temperance* (self-control): *against such there is no law* [Gal. 5:22–23].

This love that Paul speaks about has God as its primary author and expresses itself in implicit obedience to His commandments.

> *If ye love me, keep my commandments* [John 14:15].

> *Jesus answered and said unto him, If a man love me, he will keep my words: and my Father will love him, and we will come unto him, and make our abode* (home) *with him* [John 14:23].

> *If ye keep my commandments, ye shall abide in my love; even as I have kept my Father's commandments, and abide in his love* [John 15:10].
>
> *For this is the love of God, that we keep his commandments: and his commandments are not grievous* (burdensome) [1 John 5:3].
>
> *And this is love, that we walk after* (according to) *his commandments* [2 John 1:6].

Contrary to this is the self-will, or the self-pleasing approach, that negates the love of God and our love toward Him.

The love Paul speaks about is not an impulse from the feelings, nor an expression from natural inclinations, nor given only to those for whom there is some affinity. This love seeks the welfare of all. It seeks to work no ill to anyone. Paul says to the Romans,

> *Love worketh* (does no harm) *no ill to his neighbor: therefore love is the fulfilling of the law* [Rom. 13:10].

It seeks the opportunity to

> *. . . do good unto all men, especially unto them who are of the household of faith* [Gal. 6:10].

What further can we say about this *agape* love? It is God's love towards man, and it expresses itself as follows: first, it is the deep, constant love signifying the interest of a perfect being towards entirely unworthy objects; second, it produces and fosters a reverential love in the objects toward the Giver, and a practical love toward those who are partakers of it; and, third, it is a desire to help others to seek the Giver.

Go back to the question: what is meant by the phrase *speaking the truth in love*? First of all, what is not meant? It does not mean to speak lovingly, or to accept or smile upon all viewpoints or doctrinal statements.

It does not mean to put life, or spirit, or niceness, or anything else before the truth. Because if we do, we are denying essential New Testament teachings. Such an approach sets our own standards as the authority, not Scripture, the Word of God.

It is important, though it may not be the most pleasant thing, to hear that niceness, friendliness, and sentimental notions of brotherliness do not constitute Christianity, or mean someone is a member of the body of Christ. These qualities can be evident in people who are not members of the body or who even deny it. However, you cannot have Christianity, or be members of Christ's body, without accepting the truth that is *in Christ*.

Remember, this fifteenth verse begins with the word *But*. Therefore, we are to interpret this verse as being in contrast to the fourteenth verse.

We are not to be *children, tossed to and fro*. We are not to turn like weather vanes as the wind changes. We are to hold to something particular and definite. We are to hold to the truth. Clasping, professing, and walking in the truth is the very antithesis of being . . . *carried about with every wind of doctrine; by the sleight* (trickery) *of men, and cunning craftiness* [Eph. 4:14].

The questions arise: How are we to grasp the truth in love? What does the Apostle mean? Obviously, he is referring to something that can be defined. On the other hand, you cannot lay hold to something which is as nebulous, vague, or indefinite as the wind.

This whole question is interesting and applicable to our present situation. During the last century and early into this one there has been and continues to be emphases upon brotherhood, fellowship, friendliness, unity, and eliminating any divisions that separate different denominations or groups. Consequently, interpretations have been presented and accepted which describe Christianity, or in reality the teachings of Christ, as being vague, a moral code, goodwill, philosophy, or philanthropy. How can these statements and pronouncements be reconciled with what the Apostle says to the Ephesians (and to us)?

Some modern ideas deny not only Scripture but the history of the church since the Apostolic Age. The history of the church over the ages reveals the development of creeds and confessions. We have The Apostles' Creed, The Nicene Creed, The Confessions of Faith, The 39 Articles of the Church of England, the Westminster Confession of Faith, The Augsburg Confession, and The Heidelberg Confession.

How did the Creeds and Confessions come into being? These documents were developed in order to define the truth concerning the Lord Jesus Christ, to preserve the life of the church, and to inform the people.

False teachings and errors crept in and were accepted. Therefore, statements amplifying upon or stating the truth were regarded as being necessary by the leaders of the church at that time. As a result the leaders would meet and be blessed by the Holy Spirit in developing a significant statement of the truth.

However, note one thing. These individuals came together to affirm Christian doctrine (the essence of Christian truth); those who could not accept the basic tenets of the faith were not to be counted as members of Christ's body. They believed those refusing to subscribe to these truths should be rejected, not accepted. Further, they believed that the areas of uncertainty or false teachings must be eliminated. They would not compromise on the truth as revealed by the Lord Jesus who said, *I am the way, the truth, and the life* [John 14:6].

The creeds were developed to define what must be believed, and to draw a sharp distinction between right and wrong, truth and error. You cannot grasp the truth unless you know what it is. Certain doctrines or teachings are essential to the Christian faith and membership in Christ's body.

The one and only authority is the Bible. Without it you cannot discriminate between truth and error. Think of this: If the Bible is not acknowledged as the one and only authority, then *every wind of doctrine* is permissible. If that is the case, then there is no Christian faith and consequently no salvation.

There must be no question about the person of the Lord Jesus Christ. He is fully God and fully man.

The early followers, the early church, and the Reformers saw the importance of doctrine based upon the teachings of Jesus contained in the New Testament. There must be no discussion about the fact that the Lord Jesus Christ, the Son of God, is the only mediator between God and man. There is to be no argument about Him, His Person, His birth, His ministry, His atonement, and His resurrection.

The church is in her present condition because Christ's teachings and the revelation of the truth have been denied. The truth as revealed in Scripture has been replaced by philosophy, modern thought, personal experiences, or situations in the secular world.

Instead of scriptural expositions, there are philosophical attempts to try to find and define God. This approach has replaced Biblical doctrine by embracing vague teachings about God, brotherliness, Christlikeness, charitable contributions, and love based upon philosophical writings or man's secular mindset. There can be no sound teaching unless the preacher or teacher knows the truth as it is revealed by Christ and the Holy Spirit. Pastors and teachers are to speculate about neither God nor the Lord Jesus Christ. They are to proclaim the truths revealed in Scripture. Paul instructs Timothy explicitly, and in turn all professing Christians, with the following command: *And the things that thou hast heard of me among many witnesses, the same commit thou to faithful men, who shall be able to teach others also* [2 Tim. 2:2].

The message is to be the precise truth about God, the Lord Jesus Christ, the Holy Ghost, the way of salvation, and a right relationship with God the Father.

Although the Apostle wants us to hold the truth in love, he does not mean that we are to be hard, rigid, legalistic, or self-righteous. We are never to behave in such a way that any one would have the impression that our primary concern or objective is to prove we are right and everyone else is wrong.

The truth the Apostle proclaims is never to be approached with the intellect only. The heart also is to be moved by the truth. This truth is to grab our heart as well as our intellect. The truth is to be proclaimed clearly and precisely with humility, helping the hearers grasp the Word of God and grow spiritually. We do not want to even insinuate that we are right and they are wrong, but only present the truth and have the Holy Spirit interpret it aright in their hearts. We are to expound upon Scripture with compassion, love, understanding, and great patience. We are to express the truth and allow the Holy Spirit to reveal it to the hearers so that they will grasp it and accept it. We are to enlighten them. Error is to be exposed!

Truth does count. What we believe is important. *But speaking the truth in love* is more important. The love about which Paul speaks is not sentimental and weak. It is strong, true, and pure. This love desires the very best for a person. Sometimes it hurts,

> FOR WHOM THE LORD LOVETH HE CHASTENETH, AND SCOURGETH EVERY SON WHOM HE RECEIVETH [Heb. 12:6].

This love is anxious for others to be free from error and false teachings. This love will at times speak severely, it will chastise, it will rebuke, yet it will do so with love and compassion. This love does not mean that we smile at everything, that we are indulgent, or that we say everything is okay. This love is so powerful that it is prepared to hurt in order to win and to save the object of its love. This love thinks of the other party.

Paul wrote strongly to the Galatians, yet he loved them and respected them. However, there was a time when he had to remonstrate them because they had turned back to their "pagan past and did service to false Gods. In effect, do not even dare to turn again to the weak and beggarly elements! (i.e. the law). The law is described as weak because it cannot save, and it is depicted as beggarly (poor) because, as a system, it is inferior to the New Covenant," as appropriately described in *The King James Study Bible*.

These verses reveal the mind of Paul and his gentleness, but also his strong allegiance to the Lord Jesus Christ and the truth revealed in Him. As a wise pastor and preacher Paul considered not only the things that his flock may have done in error, but what can be done to bring them back to the ways of Christ. He points things out to them, but he commands them with gentleness and patience.

. . . for I am as ye are: ye have not injured me at all [Gal. 4:12] reveals that he seeks nothing but to behave kindly to them, and that they should be teachable and obedient to the Lord Jesus Christ. Then he points out that they did him no wrong, because he did not want them to think that he was avenging any injuries or a private quarrel, or twisting something into an unfavorable meaning.

Paul lets them know that he loves them, so they would hear what he had to say reminding them that since they had begun well, they should return to and continue on the same course.

These reminiscences reveal two things: his friendliness and an exhortation to act as they had at first. Then he says, *Am I therefore become your enemy, because I tell you the truth* [Gal. 4:16]? This is the same word for truth as found in Ephesians 4:15.

Paul denies it was his fault that they had changed their minds. He says this after reminding them what they would have done for him, saying, *Ye would have plucked out your own eyes, and have given them to me* [Gal. 4:15].

We all know that at times truth begets hatred, yet truth is never hateful except through the wickedness and malice of those who cannot bear to hear it. His advice is friendly, because they know him to be worthy of the love which they had previously bestowed upon him.

Then, Paul says *My little children* [Gal. 4:19]. He uses this term of endearment. Yet at the same time he suggests the tender years of those who ought to be growing as members of Christ's body. The brevity of this statement reveals Paul's strong feelings for the Galatians, because powerful emotion chokes off our speech or utterance. He follows this with further words of endearment, describing his innermost feelings with these meaningful words, *I travail* (labor) *in birth again until Christ be formed in you* [Gal. 4:19]. He means that Christ being formed in us is the same as our being formed *in Christ*. We are born again that we may become new creatures in Him.

On the other hand, Christ is born and lives in us that we may live His life. When this happens the false teachings fade from our view, and our focus is upon the Lord Jesus Christ, His authority, and His teachings. It is through Him we come to the Father and by no other way.

Amen!

20

Weaned From Milk

> *But speaking the truth in love, may grow up into him in all things, which is the head, even Christ:*
> *From whom the whole body fitly joined together and compacted* (knit together) *by that which every joint supplieth, according to the effectual* (effective) *working* (of each part doing its share) *in the measure of every part, maketh increase* (causes growth) *of the body unto the edifying of itself in love* [Eph. 4:15–16].

What did you think about when growing up? What are your memories? What positive and negative thoughts come to mind? You recall the joys and sorrows, the awkward moments; the times when you seem to know everything and then slowly but surely discover that there is so much more to learn, to discover, to experience, and about which to rejoice. What do you cherish and for what do you give thanks to almighty God?

Probably the one thing for which we do not give sufficient thanks is the blessing to develop and mature in a subject, or in certain phases of life.

Previously, we touched upon Paul addressing the Galatians as *My little children*. He was talking about their status as members of the body of Christ. He wanted them to grow, to develop, and to mature as followers of Christ. He wanted them to enjoy the fruits of the Spirit. Remember, Paul was writing to people of all ages and admonishing them to grow in their knowledge and relationship to the Lord Jesus Christ.

When examining these verses keep in mind the Apostle's concern about unity, which began in the first three verses of this chapter.

His primary objective in this fourth chapter is not doctrine, but for the believers to have a true understanding regarding the principle of unity *in Christ* and their relationship to Him. This principle becomes explicit with the words, *may grow up into him in all things, which is the Head, even Christ* [Eph. 4:15].

Regardless of our age in years, we are to *grow up*. We are to continue growing individually and collectively so that the entire body may become more mature and eventually attain . . . *unto the measure of the stature of the fullness of Christ* [Eph. 4:13].

For the Christian, there is no such thing as retiring from the study of Scripture. When Dr. McKay, the former president of Princeton Seminary, was in his nineties he was still studying, doing research, expounding Scripture and the teachings of the Lord Jesus Christ.

Questions have been asked:

- What is meant by "growing up" unto Christ?
- How can the body "grow up" into the Head, which is Christ?
- How do we explain the metaphor that Paul uses?

Scripture consistently emphasizes the importance of balance in the Christian life. If the growth results in either underdeveloped or overdeveloped parts, then there is a lack of symmetry, and the body is ugly or deformed.

We are to grow in our minds, our understanding, our hearts, our feelings, our sensibilities, and our emotions. Our growth is to be towards the surpassing perfection of Christ, and we are to grow in union with Him. Paul makes it clear in these two verses that Christ is the source and center of all activity regarding the growth of the church, His body.

Then the Apostle makes it clear that all the parts must work together. Further, not only the pastors and teachers but all the members of the church must contribute to the growth and perfection of Christ's body. Paul stresses our respective responsibilities with emphasis on the importance of love, stating,

> . . . *the whole body fitly joined together and compacted* (knit together) *by that which every joint supplieth, according to the effectual* (effective) *working in the measure of every part* (each part doing its share), *maketh increase* (causes growth) *of the body unto the edifying of itself in love* [Eph. 4:16].

The Gospel of Jesus Christ has various attractions to different people. However, the question is: does the truth of the gospel grasp us more than ever before? If the answer is not a resounding yes, then there is something wrong, something lacking.

Our understanding of the Gospel is to continuously increase. To understand the truth *in Christ* is to be moved by it and pursue more knowledge. The more familiar we become with Christ, the better we know Him, the more we understand the Master, the more we love Him. We are to grow up into Him in all things.

By now, we may agree that Paul emphasizes the importance of growing, learning, studying, understanding, and maturing as members of Christ's body. One of the prayers I have is that God will send the Holy Spirit to motivate members of Christ's body to learn more of the Word and the truth in Jesus Christ.

When thinking we have learned much, remember God is ready to give us more. Is that not one of the wonderful things about the Gospel? The more we learn, the more we want to learn, and the more knowledge God wants to bestow upon us. We should remember that we are like jars, only partially filled, and will never be filled fully. Paul provides the Corinthians with sage advice for not continuing to live as babes in their thinking and conduct, but as responsible disciples of the Lord Jesus Christ, when he admonishes them with the following words,

> *Brethren, be not children in understanding: howbeit in malice be ye children* (babes), *but in understanding be men* (mature) [1 Cor. 14:20].

From this statement it is apparent that malice, evil, and ill will are to become less and less evident in our lives, but understanding is to grow, grow, and grow. How can it grow unless it is nourished?

The Apostle Paul says something incisive on this subject. He goes back to Isaiah and draws understanding and enlightenment from his words. He tells the Corinthians that they are not to seek after something God considers accursed. Paul reminds them that the Prophet Isaiah made a strong attack on the ten tribes and became upset over the corruption of Judah. There was no hope for improvement in any of them. Consequently he said, *Whom shall he teach knowledge? and whom shall he make to understand doctrine* (the message)?*them that are* (just) *weaned from the milk, and* (just) *drawn from the breasts* [Isa. 28:9].

What does Isaiah mean? He means that the adult Israelites are no more capable of instruction than newly weaned infants. What a condemnation!

The Prophet Isaiah adds hard words upon hard words, saying in a mimicking tone, *. . . here a little, and there a little* [Isa. 28:10].

He brings out their slowness, their reluctance, their self-centeredness, and their complacency. He is unhappy because they are not making progress. Isaiah continues, saying, *For with stammering lips and another tongue will he speak to this people* [Isa. 28:11]. That is a direct and illuminating statement.

What do the prophets and apostles mean? That the people are afflicted with such blindness and folly, that when God speaks to them they do not understand it any better than a barbarian or foreigner would understand another language. Isaiah concluded the section by saying, *. . . yet they would not hear* [Isa. 28:12]. What a condemning statement! They would not hear the Lord, their God! Paul wanted the Corinthians to understand not only his words, but Isaiah's.

The conclusion Paul draws is: brethren, be not like children. Why? Because this means that God's message may resound in your ears, but there will be no positive results. Therefore, you will reject prophecy, you will reject the truth. The result will be that you will not receive the blessings of God, but "You are heading straight for the curse of God," as John Calvin states in unmistakenly strong language.

Have you noticed how Paul anticipates the Corinthians, that some of them may say it is praiseworthy to be children spiritually? He says be children in malice, but in your thinking be adults. Paul wants all believers to be mature in their thinking and understanding.

> *Now I beseech you, brethren, mark* (note) *them which cause divisions and offences contrary to the doctrine which ye have learned; and avoid them.*
> *For they that are such serve not our Lord Jesus Christ, but their own belly; and by good* (flattering) *words and fair* (innocent) *speeches deceive the hearts of the simple* [Rom. 16:17–18].

Paul does not want the Romans distracted from the unity of the truth. He knows that the truth of God can be distorted or destroyed by human teachings or inventions. He exhorts us to beware and to be responsible. He does not want us to be deceived or caught unawares. Often our neglect or ignorance causes harm to Christ's body.

Note, Paul is speaking to those who had been taught God's pure truth. He was not addressing nonbelievers or recent members of the fellowship.

The Romans are praised for their obedience. Then Paul says, . . . *but yet I would have you wise unto that which is good, and simple concerning evil* [Rom. 16:19]. What a wonderful statement! May we grasp it, thank him for it, and apply it.

Paul extols a certain character of simplicity in Christians, but not to those who regard a lack of knowledge, or stupid ignorance of the Word of God, as a virtue. They are not to lay claim to such a title. Paul commends the Romans for being obedient and receptive; however, he wants them to exercise wisdom and discernment. He wants them to act with prudence and care and to recognize imposters.

Scripture, both the Old Testament and the New Testament, reveals we are to grow and to mature *in Christ*. We are to develop in Him, and we are to conform to Him.

Each of us, regardless of our knowledge or capabilities, is to *grow up* into Christ. We are to realize that we receive our life, our light, and our strength from Christ. The question is, why? The reason we receive these blessings is not merely for ourselves, but to minister to others. We may have no official office or function to perform, but we are to grow, serve, and witness.

Probably the fifteenth and sixteenth verses of this fourth chapter are among the most complicated the Apostle ever wrote. He appears to be bringing to a conclusion the theme of unity among members of the body of Christ. Further, he wanted to include everything he had presented in order to provide the Ephesians (and us) a complete picture of the truths being considered.

He states that the Head is Christ. Any consideration of the body, or the church, must focus on the Head, and that is Christ. Christ is the Head of the church. He is the source of all her life, her energy, and her growth. Without Him there is no church, and there could not be one.

Paul makes two statements concerning the believers *in Christ*. He says they are *fitly joined together* and *compacted*. The former means several parts bound together. The Greek word for *joined* means "to lay systematically together." We are members of the body and systematically put together. The ideal condition of the church, as with the body, is that every member fits together with every other member and in so doing preserves . . . *the unity of the spirit in the bond of peace* [Eph. 4:3].

The latter term *compacted* means "closely knit" or "brought and held together." The Greek word for *compacted* is *symbibazo* and it means "to raise up together."

How is it brought into being, and how is it maintained? The answers to these questions are found in one of the Apostle's most difficult phrases. Therefore, we must carefully consider the words he uses and their meaning.

First, he says *by that which every joint supplieth*. *Joint* in this verse means "fitting together." It can mean a connecting link or a band, enabling the different parts to fit together. This term means not only fitting together or uniting, it also means that through these connecting links flows the supplies of life and energy. It is through the bands that the life and energy flow.

Second is the term *supply*. It means an abundant supply or super abundance, not merely a sufficiency. The same idea is in

> . . . *the exceeding riches of his grace* [Eph. 2:7].

> *And to know the love of Christ, which passeth knowledge, that ye might be filled with all the fullness of God* [Eph. 3:19].

Third is the *effectual* (effective) *working*. This term means the inner working, the energy that does something. Each part of the body does not receive the same amount, but each part receives all it needs according to the measure of its capacity.

All parts of the body, the eye, head, foot, nose, tongue, and ear, are not of equal importance, but they are all members of the body and are essential to its working.

Why is the body constructed as it is? Why is the church, or body of Christ, constituted as it is?

The objective is the increased growth of the body and its capabilities. The church has been formed so that it may grow. That is why it is *fitly joined together*, why it has an abundant *supply*, and why there is an *effectual working* of all the parts. The purpose is to promote growth and to build up the body. *For the perfecting* (equipping) *of the saints, for the work of the ministry, for the edifying of the body of Christ* [Eph. 4:12]. Nothing is more important than love in this matter of unity. If the head is love, then the body must be love. The body is to conform to the head. The body is to *grow up* in love.

What enables the body to function? The head contains the brain and the whole nervous system is connected to it. The smallest nerve or nerve tendril can be traced back to the brain. The nervous system links the whole body together. The same thing can be said of the vascular system.

Therefore, the Apostle says the supply, the origin of life, the energy, the power and sustenance, and all that is needed is in the Head, which is Christ. From there it passes to every part of the body.

Paul says we are all dependent upon the Head. He alone is the source of supply. "Yet at the same time, if there is any defect in any part, then the development and functioning of the whole is interrupted and rendered imperfect," as stated by Martyn Lloyd Jones. The individual parts are important and contribute to the whole.

The Apostle teaches that if the whole body is to grow, to develop, to function, and to build itself up in love, then each part must be filled to its capacity with an abundant supply and work effectually. Each member is vitally important.

Paul shows the glory of the body, the church, and of each member. It is a privilege to be a member of the body. These questions we must ask ourselves, contemplate, and endeavor to answer honestly as members of Christ's body:

- Are we growing and developing our capacity?
- Are we fulfilling our function?
- Are we performing our functions as members of the body?
- Are we causing pain or trouble to other parts of the body?
- Are we being lazy or lethargic?
- Are we putting a part before the whole?

Remember *that we henceforth be no more children*. We are to develop and to grow into Him who is the Head, even Christ.

What does all this have to do with unity *in Christ*? Each part is to perform and discharge its duties. However, each part is to support and help every other part as well as the whole.

The pastors and teachers are to discover by prayer and meditation what God has revealed to them, and they are to share it with others. They are to present the teachings of Christ and pray that the Holy Spirit will illuminate our hearts and minds. The officers and members also have their functions to perform.

It is the devoutness, charity, uprightness, and zeal of the members that contribute to the force and impact of the church. It is exhibited in different ways, such as cheerfulness in facing adversity, poverty, and infirmities; faithfulness despite obstacles or temptations; love despite rejection or ill will; not succumbing to the temptations of the flesh and mind; refraining from responding to attacks, resentment, injustices, and unkindnesses; and being children in malice, but adults in understanding. It is further evident by obedience instead of license; growing in knowledge; reverence, not irreverence; caring for others; exercising heartfelt forgiveness; and producing the fruit of the Spirit. The unity Paul describes is a unity of life. It is not a unity of organizations.

This unity is created by the Spirit of God. It is not the unity of ecclesiastical statesmanship. The unity of the Spirit exists despite differences of policy or creed. It exists in the body of Christ. It exists in the *One Lord, one faith, one baptism*, and in the *One God and Father of all*.

This unity does not merely exist. It has manifested itself throughout the centuries. It manifests itself through the remarkable unity of doctrine and the teachings of the Old Testament and Christ.

The unity of the church is seen not only in its love, but in the love exhibited by the Lord Jesus Christ. His love is shown in many forms. He admonished, He corrected, He gave, He forgave, He instructed, and He obeyed. We are to increase in spiritual knowledge and in knowing the love of Christ, so that we will increase in love. Our works are useless if they do not produce love. Therefore, let us . . . *maketh increase* (causes growth) *of the body unto the edifying of itself in love* [Eph. 4:16].

Amen!

21

Spirit Producing Fruit

> *But speaking the truth in love, may grow up into him in all things, which is the head, even Christ:*
> *From whom the whole body fitly joined together and compacted* (knit together) *by that which every joint supplieth, according to the effectual* (effectively) *working* (of each part doing its share) *in the measure of every part, maketh increase* (causes growth) *of the body unto the edifying of itself in love* [Eph. 4:15–16].

There is a sense in which this section of Scripture is one of the most relevant portions of the holy Word in these days. Undoubtedly, it will be just as relevant in the next century, and to our children's children and their descendants. The truths contained in these verses are intensely practical and relevant to a person alone with his or her own thoughts, a person walking through life with other people, and a person having a relationship with our Lord Jesus Christ and God the Father.

Remember, the people to whom this letter was written. They were followers in the Way, not the other residents of Ephesus. They were to intelligently understand Scripture and the Lord Jesus Christ. They were not to be carried away by *every wind of doctrine*, or vague generalities, or a sentimental interest. And they were to have a . . . *unity of the Spirit in the bond of peace* [Eph. 4:3].

Another reason for emphasizing these principles and truths is to understand what has been happening to the body of Christ, the church and its members.

We are to acquire knowledge so we can deal with different situations and controversial matters. Above all we are to walk with Christ and have a personal relationship with Him that grows and grows.

Therefore, we must face difficulties as we encounter and examine them. How? In the light of Scripture. When considering these matters, it may be well to keep in mind Paul's words to Timothy, *For God hath not given us the spirit of fear; but of power, and of love, and of a sound mind* [2 Tim. 1:7]. Paul urges Timothy to give evidence of the gifts and power he has received.

We are endowed with power from on high. God equips us with the Spirit of His power. It is by this that we see and recognize the majesty of God. It enables us to see the truth *in Christ* and to grasp it. In these verses, Paul states that the powerful energy of the Spirit is tempered by love and a sound mind. Sound mind means edification, enlightenment, and self-control.

The Apostle starts the first sixteen verses of Ephesians Chapter 4 with the principle of unity. There is to be unity in the body of Christ, for "organic unity in the body, is what makes it a body," as stated by Martyn Lloyd-Jones.

The questions may be asked: What brings unity into being? And, what hinders unity?

First, never think of unity in the church as only an external, mechanical, or organizational manner. It is not something you add or attach. It is not a collection of parts. The illustration of the body makes that quite clear!

Second, unity is never achieved by merely removing divisions. This is brought up in the context that there are divisions in the church, which is a tragedy.

How do we eliminate the divisions? This is a negative approach because it presumes if you remove the divisions you will have unity. If there are divisions between the hand and foot, or ear and nose, or arm and leg, you will not achieve unity by removing one of them.

The principle of unity is never to be placed first, because unity is not something in and of itself. It is always the result of something else. Since we are not to start with unity, where do we start? With the nature of the church! Then we will see that unity is inevitable. The body itself is of primary importance, and unity is but one characteristic of the body.

These principles are absolutely basic to the whole matter of unity. It may sound radical, but let the leaders of large denominations and groupings be what they are and do what they want with respect to large organizations. However, our business and our efforts should be directed toward discovering the real nature of the Christian church, the body of Christ.

Think of Martin Luther. Despite overwhelming odds, with respect to his background, his environment, his education, and his commitment, he was restless and he was searching. Undoubtedly, he was praying and seeking God's guidance. In so doing, he focused on the living Word of God, Scripture. We do not know how long he wrestled, but we do know that it was with God's revealed Word, not with the opinions of men and his existing mindset. There you have it: praying to God; searching Scripture; and seeking God's truth. What happened? The Holy Spirit revealed God's truth and satisfied his quest. We must do the same. We are not to allow our thinking to be determined by the present situation or our own mindset. Two questions should be addressed: What is the true nature of the church? What determines unity?

"The first essential is true belief in the Lord Jesus Christ. The Apostle does not begin to talk about *endeavoring to keep the unity of the Spirit in the bond of peace* at the beginning of his letter. He does not bring that up until the fourth chapter, after he has laid down the great fundamental truths of the faith. That is Paul's approach. How different it is today when men preach unity instead of preaching Christ. Some preach the church instead of preaching salvation. They talk of what they are doing instead of what Christ has done and is doing.

"Why is this so? Because they do not realize that unity results from something else and is the consequence of something else.

"When re-examining the fifteenth verse which begins, *But speaking the truth in love*, please note what comes first *the truth*, and second *in love*. We are to speak the truth first. Why? It is impossible to discuss unity with a person who denies the deity of Christ. . . . We cannot have unity with such a person. We both must be rooted and grounded in the truth," as expressly stated by Martin Lloyd-Jones. The truth is Jesus Christ, and it is in Him!

We must believe the truths taught in the first three chapters of this Epistle before we can have unity. They are the sovereignty of God, the unique deity of Christ, the shedding of His blood for the remission of our sins, being dead in trespasses and sins, the lusts of the flesh and the mind, and the children of wrath.

These facts are vital. These truths and the other basic teachings of Christ and His apostles are of primary importance. It is not important that someone says he was born in a certain country or of a certain family that makes him a Christian, or that he was baptized. The truths presented by Paul are at the core of our relationship to Christ and each other.

The Apostle Paul said *speaking the truth in love*. However, we must recognize that we cannot have or maintain *the unity of the Spirit in the bond of peace* if we disagree about the basic truths of Christ's teachings and His being: the virgin birth; the miracles; the atoning, sacrificial death; the resurrection of our Lord; and the person of the Holy Spirit. Note, the Apostle states, *For through Him we both* (Jew and Gentile) *have access by one Spirit unto the Father* [Eph. 2:18]. That is the only way! Hopefully, you understand that we cannot talk about unity or having it until we agree on these basic truths.

The second principle is that we are to have a right relationship with our Lord, and our union is to be with Him. We are to understand this doctrine of a relationship with the Lord Jesus Christ. This union with Him is not a matter of organizations. It is a question of being a branch in the vine, being a member of His body.

If we understand that the church is the body of Christ then we should accept this doctrine. The basic question is not can I have fellowship with this person or that, but am I and is he or she *in Christ*? Are we branches of the same vine?

Third, consider the life that is in the body. The life of the Spirit in the individual and the collective members. The life must come before unity, because unity is the result of life. What produces and maintains the organic unity of a body? Life.

What does the Apostle say?

> *But speaking the truth in love, may grow up into him in all things, which is the head, even Christ:*
> *From whom the whole body fitly joined together and compacted* (knit together) *by that which every joint supplieth, according to the effectual* (effective) *working in the measure of every part* (each part doing its share)*, maketh increase* (causes growth) *of the body unto the edifying of itself in love.*

What does our Lord and Master say? *I am the way, the truth and the life: no man cometh unto the Father, but by me* [John 14:6]. We are to understand that truth and accept it.

However, there is a difference between being active in the life of the church and the life *in Christ*, just as there is between *the works of the flesh* and *the fruit of the spirit* as noted by Paul in his letter to the Galatians.

> *Now the works of the flesh . . . are these; adultery, fornication, uncleanness, lasciviousness* (licentiousness),
> *Idolatry, witchcraft* (sorcery), *hatred, variance* (contentions), *emulations* (jealousies), *wrath, strife* (self ambitions), *seditions* (dissensions), *heresies,*
> *Envyings, murders, drunkenness, revellings, and such like:* . . . *that they which do such things shall not inherit the kingdom of God.*
> *But the fruit of the Spirit is love, joy, peace, long-suffering, gentleness* (kindness), *goodness, faith* (faithfulness),
> *Meekness, temperance* (self-control): *against such there is no law* [Gal. 5:19-23].

There is a distinct difference between the *works of the flesh* and *the fruit of the spirit*. It is easy to grasp the difference between them. "The flesh works, it produces work as a machine does; but the spirit produces fruit as a tree does," as simply, yet effectively, expressed by Martyn Lloyd-Jones. The blessings of the Spirit are the result of life and growth.

There is a distinction between activity and life in a church. There can be activity almost every day and night in a church, but that does not mean there is life in the Spirit. There can be activities such as clubs, dramatic presentations, sports, entertainment, and dancing, but that does not mean there is life.

On the other hand, I fondly remember the First Presbyterian Church in Pittsburgh where there were study groups, teacher training courses, worship services, Bible classes, or smaller functions every day, but there was life in the Spirit in that congregation in addition to the various activities.

During most of the twentieth century there was an emphasis upon preserving the church as an institution and extolling the works of the church. There was an emphasis upon external appearances, the number of members, and finances. The debt on churches and buildings has been lower than ever. Isn't that wonderful? (I say so facetiously.)

What is the spiritual condition of the churches? What about witnessing and the growth of the body of Christ? Yes, the finances are sounder for many churches of the different denominations in general, but the approach has been wrong.

The institutional idea has dominated the thinking of the organized church. They have tried to appeal to those who do not like sermons, especially expository ones, by providing drama, entertainment, and games.

Why has this approach been taken? Because there has been a failure to understand the doctrine of the church as the body of Christ. The New Testament makes it evident that Christ is the life of the church, and if there is not a vital relationship with Him there will be no church.

For the most part, the church at large is interested in numbers and is convinced that if we could eliminate denominational barriers and divisions, that would end many of the problems confronting the institutional church. Further, if we were one large church, the world would listen to us, and consequently, we would be able to do marvelous things.

I remember a minister telling me how wonderful it was when the Presbyterian Church United States and the United Presbyterian Church decided to merge. I asked, "Why?" He said, "Because we will be X million in number, look how large we will be." That was his reason. (Time has proven him wrong.)

The idea that size is what counts is a contradiction of what the whole Bible teaches. The Old Testament has one doctrine running through it. The doctrine of *the remnant*. See how our modern thinking has parted from Scripture.

We need to remember and be aware of the fact that our Lord Jesus Christ left the church in the hands of twelve men. A mere handful of nobodies. We do not emphasize that! As a matter of fact, we seem to forget it!

What about Martin Luther? He stood alone against the Roman Catholic Church, against the centuries of deadness, against all the powers arrayed against him, and look what happened. Why? Because he was a member of the body, and the power and life of the Head were in him.

What matters in the church is not numbers. What matters is our relationship to Him, the purity of our doctrine, the purity of our life and living, and whether we are witnesses to Him and for Him. As Jesus says, *for without me ye can do nothing* [John 15:5]. We must realize this truth as members of the body of Christ.

"It is the Head who acts. The body does not act. Of course, we all know that the head acts through the body, but nevertheless it is the head that acts and controls. The head decides and determines when, where, and how to act. The head is the originator and the initiator. We, as members of the body, are the channels through which the activities pass," as expressed by Martyn Lloyd-Jones.

If we studiously look back over the last century, we will find that there has been much activity, but most of it has been by the members, not the head. Therefore, questions should be asked:

- What is the nature and character of our activities?
- What is the value of them in our relationship to Christ?
- How do they proclaim the glory of God?
- Do they produce the results that Christ would have us produce?

These are questions to be asked when considering the status of a single church and the organized church at large.

Is it possible that organizations and activities mislead us? What has happened to the church? This is a vital question. Once that is asked, hopefully it will lead to asking basic, fundamental questions: Why are we in our current position? Why is attendance off? Why is the position of the church not as strong as it once was? These questions should lead to asking certain vital ones:

- Has our doctrine been right?
- Have we been ministering to the real needs of the community of believers?
- Have we been proclaiming the Gospel?
- Have we been presenting the teachings of Jesus Christ?
- Have we been presenting the deity of Christ, the virgin birth, the miracles, the truth as it is found in Jesus Christ, the substitutionary atonement, the Cross, the shedding of His blood, and the bodily resurrection?
- Have we been doing these things?
- Have we spent sufficient time in prayer regarding these matters?

Our first task is to examine ourselves in the light of the Gospel and the teachings of Christ. It is to be done on this basis, not what is done in business, social clubs, or other external entities. When we do this we will pray for the Lord to send His Spirit to revive us, and to strengthen us with His power and might.

We need to pray for true revival and pray for it continuously. We need to start with prayer and discovering God's will. He opens doors; He makes things possible. But we need to put ourselves at His disposal and wait for Him to act. Remember, it is the Head who decides to act and causes action.

When there is real revival, not just evangelistic campaigns, then there is a period of success, true growth, and progress according to the teachings of Christ. Revival means being firmly bound to the Head which is Christ, receiving from Him, and placing ourselves joyfully at His disposal.

Now we come to the final principle. What is it? It is the call of the New Testament. It does not call us to do things, but to be something. We are to be something, we are to be useable, we are to submit ourselves to the will of God, and we are to respond to the call by learning and doing.

In this call, and in response to this command, there are several developments that may occur. They have occurred to some of the great servants of God such as the Wesley brothers, Jonathan Edwards, and George Whitefield. The following words describe what they experienced and what happens to those who become members of Christ's body:

- first, there is an intense struggle within the person, and a reliance upon his or her own powers and abilities;
- then, there is the realization of the person's need for a greater power and greater strength, followed by submission to the Lord Jesus Christ and being filled with the Holy Spirit; and
- third, there is the completion process of being baptized with the Holy Spirit and His power, and going out as a person transformed and doing amazing things.

Such individuals are used to revive the church and build up the people of God.

Hopefully, you see from this that it is for God to act, and for us to follow His teachings and obey His commands. Therefore, during our trials and tribulations as well as our periods of usefulness we are not to ask what can I do next, but what would God have me to do. How can I be filled according to the measure of my capacity? We are to pray that God will fill us with His Spirit.

Yes, we should pray for revival, we should pray to be witnesses, we should pray to be used by God in His way, and we should pray that His power comes upon us and into us.

Remember, Christ said,

> *I am the vine, ye are the branches: He that abideth in me, and I in him, the same bringeth forth much fruit: for without me ye can do nothing* [John 15:5].

May we abide in Him and bring forth much fruit! May we be something for Him, Christ Jesus!

Amen!

Outline Questions

Chapter 1

Prisoner of the Lord

> *I THEREFORE, the prisoner of the Lord, beseech you that ye walk worthy of the vocation* (calling) *wherewith ye are called,*
>   *With all lowliness and meekness* (gentleness), *with longsuffering, forbearing* (bearing with) *one another in love;*
>   *Endeavoring to keep the unity of the Spirit in the bond of peace* [Eph. 4:1–3].

What are our responsibilities when we know and believe God's truths as they are revealed to us?

Why does Paul always consider doctrine and practice together?

What does Paul mean by using the word *therefore*?

What are the differences between Paul's lofty, powerful prayer at the end of the third chapter and his passages at the beginning of the fourth chapter?

How does Paul connect faith and righteousness with our individual responsibilities?

What characteristics does Paul exhort us to exhibit?

What does Paul put first?

How does one receive humility?

How is meekness exhibited?

What traits did Paul realize people would exhibit?

What factors should we exhibit as we embark on our walk with Christ?

What does Paul tell us about the nature and character of the life we are to live?

Chapter 2

Regeneration

> *Jesus answered and said unto him, Verily, verily, I say unto thee, Except a man be born again* (from above), *he cannot see the kingdom of God.*
> *Nicodemus saith unto him, How can a man be born when he is old? can he enter the second time into his mother's womb, and be born?*
> *Jesus answered, Verily, verily, I say unto thee, Except a man be born of water and of the Spirit, he cannot enter into the kingdom of God* [John 3:3–5].

What teachings of Paul's are not part of our sanctification?

What does sanctification mean?

What other terms are used for sanctification? Why?

What does the Doctrine of Justification describe?

What happens when God justifies us?

What is our assurance that all our sins have been forgiven?

How are good works viewed with respect to salvation?

How did the Reformation view *good works*?

What does Paul say about the "work of faith"?

What do good works have to do with justification?

How is a person justified?

What do the words just, justify, and justification mean?

What is the Reformation's thrust regarding justification?

What does it mean for a person to become right?

What two conditions are necessary for justification?

Chapter 3

Called to Walk in His Footsteps

I THEREFORE, the prisoner of the Lord, beseech you that ye walk worthy of the vocation (calling) *wherewith ye are called, . . .* [Eph. 4:1].

What is the foundation for the last three chapters of Ephesians?

Where does a true understanding of doctrine lead one?

What did Paul want the Ephesians (and us) to know?

How can you perform properly in a chosen discipline or field without knowing the details?

What does the word "*walk*" imply?

How does God want us to *walk*?

What is required to *walk worthy*?

What type of *walk* is it?

What does the word *worthy* mean?

Why are we to "show . . . diligence to the *full assurance of hope unto the end*"?

What are we called to do?

What are we to become?

What is the primary reason for being the *called ones*?

What are we called to believe?

What are we to remember as we proceed on our *walk*?

What truths are we to remember regarding our call to follow Christ?

Chapter 4

Unity

> *With all lowliness and meekness* (gentleness), *with longsuffering, forbearing* (bearing with) *one another in love;*
> *Endeavouring to keep the unity of the Spirit in the bond of peace* [Eph. 4:2–3].

Why does Paul stress *the unity of the Spirit*?

Why is unity important?

What is the basis for this unity?

How is unity defined and declared?

How are we to keep unity?

How is unity produced?

Why is it important for us to know Christ and to believe in Him?

How do we *keep the unity of the Spirit in the bond of peace*?

Why does God teach us and then test us?

What happens when we manifest the principles Paul presents?

What is the end of all doctrine and conduct?

What is the fruit of the Spirit?

Chapter 5

One Body, and One Spirit

> *There is one body, and one Spirit, even as ye are called in one hope of your calling;*
> *One Lord, one faith, one baptism,*
> *One God and Father of all, who is above all, and through all, and in you all* [Eph. 4:4–6].

What do we need to stress in our minds as we continue on our walk?

How does Paul handle the matter of unity?

Why does the Apostle begin with the Holy Spirit and then go to the Lord Jesus and God the Father?

What is it that the Apostle does not want us to do?

What does the Apostle mean by referring to the church as *one body*?

How does the community of believers exist?

What characteristics of the body of Christ does Weber identify?

What does Paul mean by *the cup of blessing*?

What is the significance of union with Christ?

What does believing in Christ mean?

Who brought the visible and invisible church into being?

What are we to understand about the invisible church?

What do the body's characteristics teach us about the church, the body of Christ?

How does God reveal Himself?

Chapter 6

The Person of the Holy Spirit

There is one body, and one Spirit, even as ye are called in one hope of your calling [Eph. 4:4].

What is the crux of what Paul says about the *one Spirit*?

Why is He called the Holy Spirit?

What is it that the Holy Spirit does or is doing?

How are we justified and sanctified?

Where do we find the Holy Spirit?

What does Calvin say about the Holy Spirit and His work?

How is the Spirit known?

How does Christ manifest Himself to the community of believers?

When was the Holy Spirit given?

What did the early disciples do after being converted?

What did Jesus say to His disciples when they assembled after His resurrection?

Chapter 7

The Holy Spirit

> *There is one body, and one Spirit, even as ye are called in one hope of your calling;*
> *One Lord, one faith, one baptism,*
> *One God and Father of all, who is above all, and through all, and in you all* [Eph. 4:4–6].

What is recorded in Acts regarding the Holy Spirit revealing Himself to the Gentiles?

What does the Holy Spirit do after a person realizes his or her reconciliation with God?

What does the Holy Spirit awaken within us?

What is our need regarding the Holy Ghost?

What is the reconciling work of Jesus Christ?

What does the Holy Ghost do when there is enmity?

Where and how does peace established by God permeate others?

What impact does the Holy Spirit have on our relationship with God?

What is meant by *adoption* in the New Testament?

What should we remember about standing before God?

What does Calvin say about Christ's kingly office?

What fruit does the Holy Spirit produce?

What happens when the Holy Spirit produces fruit?

How can I become something I am not at this time?

Chapter 8

Looking Forward

There is one body, and one Spirit, even as ye are called in one hope of your calling [Eph. 4:4].

What does the Holy Spirit do regarding the Lord Jesus?

Why did the Apostle add the phrase *even as ye are called in one hope of your calling*?

What is the church supposed to be?

What does Paul bring to the Ephesians' attention?

What causes divisions and misunderstandings to develop and to continue?

How do conversions occur?

What does the relationship between the Mudites and Anti-Mudites reveal?

What does Paul teach about progress and pressing forward?

Why does Christ grasp us?

What are we to forget?

What is stressed in Ephesians?

What does Paul condemn?

What does Paul say to the Philippians that applies to us?

Why does Paul press forward?

What does Paul want for members of the community of believers?

Chapter 9

King of Kings, Lord of Lords

One Lord, one faith, one baptism, . . . [Eph. 4:5].

Who did the early writers identify when using the term *one Lord*?

Who does the term *Kyrios* identify?

Who is our Master?

How does *Kyrios* differ from the title Son of God?

How is Christ's deity revealed?

How do we say Jesus is Lord?

How are we to interpret Paul's emphasis upon *one Lord*?

What is Christianity?

Where and when is the Christian faith intolerant?

What did the authorities seek to prohibit the apostles from preaching?

Who is the only one who can come between God and each of us?

How is a person ignorant of Christ?

What does Jesus emphasize regarding Himself and His disciples?

Who is the central figure in Paul's letter to the Ephesians?

Chapter 10

Thy Blood Shed for Me

One Lord, one faith, one baptism, . . . [Eph. 4:5].

What points of view are offered regarding the term *one faith*?

What does the term *one faith* mean?

What does faith in Christ mean?

What does this faith do?

What does Scripture reveal regarding *one faith*?

How does God justify the ungodly?

What does the word of faith reveal?

How long has God been bestowing His gift of righteousness?

How is a person justified?

What is the only way of salvation?

How can we break the unity described by Paul in the term *one faith*?

How can the *one faith* and one way of salvation be stated very simply?

Chapter 11

Baptism

One Lord, one faith, one baptism, ... [Eph. 4:5].

What is meant by the term baptism?

What are the essential ingredients of baptism?

What are a few negative factors to consider regarding baptism?

What is the basis for baptism?

Where is the validity of baptism?

Where does baptism have its basis?

What does *one baptism* represent and signify?

In addition to washing away our sins, what important truths does baptism represent?

Why does it mean we are confessing Christ, when we are baptized?

What is the special character of baptism?

What is incorporated into Christian baptism?

Chapter 12

God, the Father

There is one body, and one Spirit, even as ye are called in one hope of your calling;
  One Lord, one faith, one baptism,
  One God and Father of all, who is above all, and through all, and in you all [Eph. 4:4–6].

How are we transformed from being outside Christ to being *in Christ*?

Who is concerned with our salvation?

What truths can help us to understand the principle of unity?

What did Paul teach throughout his ministry?

What did Paul teach about the Godhead?

What is the objective of our salvation?

What does the Bible reveal about God and sin?

What is meant by *God the Father*?

What does the New Testament reveal about God the Father?

What does Paul mean by, *One God and Father of all, . . . above all, . . . through all, and in you all*?

How is the fatherhood of God limited?

From whom do certain truths come?

How does Paul deal with the members of the community of believers?

How has God adopted us?

What is God's eternal purpose for His children?

What is Paul telling us when he says, *God . . . is above all, and through all, and in you all*?

Chapter 13

But Unto Every One

> *But unto every one of us is given grace according to the measure of the gift of Christ.*
>
> *Wherefore he saith, WHEN HE ASCENDED UP ON HIGH, HE LED CAPTIVITY CAPTIVE, AND GAVE GIFTS UNTO MEN.*
>
> *(Now that HE ASCENDED, what is it but that he also descended first into the lower parts of the earth?*
>
> *He that descended is the same also that ascended up far above all heavens, that he might fill (fulfill) all things.*
>
> *And he (himself) gave some, apostles; and some, prophets; and some, evangelists; and some, pastors and teachers;*
>
> *For the perfecting (equipping) of the saints, for the work of the ministry, for the edifying of the body of Christ:*
>
> *Till we all come in (into) the unity of the faith, and of the knowledge of the Son of God, unto a perfect (mature) man, unto the measure of the stature of the fullness of Christ* [Eph. 4:7–13].

What is not meant by *unity* as used by Paul?

How can unity be preserved in view of diversity and variety?

To whom are spiritual blessings given?

How and why does God bestow diverse gifts upon believers?

What is the purpose of bestowing gifts upon members of the community of believers?

How are we to progress in our relationship with Christ?

What does Paul encourage us to do with the gifts we receive?

Why does the Holy Spirit distribute gifts among the members of His community?

Why does Paul digress in the seventh verse and refer us to the Sixty-eighth Psalm?

Why do some authorities say that David writes about the Lord Jesus Christ?

What is revealed about the Holy Trinity in these verses?

Why was David able to give an accurate description of what happened through the Lord Jesus Christ?

From whom do gifts come to the community of believers?

What does Paul reveal in these verses?

Chapter 14

Worship Intelligently

But unto every one of us is given grace according to the measure of the gift of Christ [Eph. 4:7].

Why are we to worship intelligently?

What traits are we to acquire in our walk with Christ?

What attitude does Paul want us to have?

What are we to do?

What did Christ do?

Who is the Lord of history?

What happens when we do not know and apply Scripture?

What did Jesus do that we might learn, know, and practice?

Why did Christ give apostles, prophets, evangelists, pastors and teachers?

What were the distinguishing characteristics of the apostles?

What was true of the prophets?

What were the traits of the evangelists?

What is true of the pastors and teachers?

Why were these gifts given?

Chapter 15

Faith and Knowledge

Till we all come in (into) *the unity of the faith, and of the knowledge of the Son of God, unto a perfect* (mature) *man, unto the measure of the stature of the fullness of Christ* [Eph. 4:13].

What does our failure to understand the true meaning of membership in the church cause?

What type church does Paul describe?

Why are the fourth to sixteenth verses of the fourth chapter important to understanding the church as the body of Christ?

How are members of Christ's body to exhibit their trust in Him?

What two things are we to attain as Christ's followers?

What does the unity of faith mean?

What knowledge does Paul want us to have regarding the unity of faith?

What does this knowledge require?

How are we to know the Lord Jesus Christ?

Upon what does unity with Christ and knowledge about Him depend?

How are our faith and knowledge to increase?

What other factors are we to examine?

What is the essence of perfection according to the Bible?

Chapter 16

The Perfect Man

Till we all come in (into) *the unity of the faith, and of the knowledge of the Son of God, unto a perfect* (mature) *man, unto the measure of the stature of the fullness of Christ* [Eph. 4:13].

What is meant by the term *a perfect man*?

What is the highest perfection of Christians?

Who is *a perfect man*?

What alternatives are to be considered regarding *a perfect man*?

What is meant by Christ's command to *Be ye . . . perfect*?

Why are we to be concerned about our union with each other?

What does the phrase mean *unto the measure of the stature of the fullness of Christ*?

In what sense is Christ's fullness not complete without us?

Outline Questions 215

What leads to problems in local congregations and the church at large?

What are we to strive to do as members of Christ's church?

Who was the most important: Lydia or Paul? Why?

Chapter 17

Henceforth

> *That we henceforth be no more children, tossed to and fro, and carried about with every wind of doctrine, by the sleight* (trickery) *of men, and cunning craftiness, whereby they lie in wait to deceive;*
> *But speaking the truth in love, may grow up into him in all things, which is the head, even Christ:*
> *From whom the whole body fitly joined together and compacted* (knit together) *by that which every joint supplieth, according to the effectual* (effective) *working in the measure of every part* (each part doing its share), *maketh increase* (causes growth) *of the body unto the edifying of itself in love* [Eph. 4:14–16].

Why did Christ give certain gifts to the apostles, prophets, evangelists, pastors and teachers?

Why does Paul use the term *henceforth*?

Why isn't there more emphasis on children in preaching and teaching?

What is significant about Nicodemus's encounter with Christ?

What is required of a person in order to grow in the Spirit?

Why does Paul use the metaphors *tossed to and fro* and *carried about*?

What are the characteristics of children?

How can we describe a child?

What does the term *sound mind* mean?

What is meant by the phrase *carried about by every wind of doctrine*?

Why can a child be imposed upon?

What happens to adults who are growing and maturing in the faith?

What is required to mature in the faith?

Chapter 18

Cunning Craftiness

> *That we henceforth be no more children, tossed to and fro, and carried about with every wind of doctrine, by the sleight (trickery) of men, and cunning craftiness, whereby they lie in wait to deceive* [Eph. 4:14].

Why don't we like warnings, rebukes, and being told we are going in the wrong direction?

What did Paul learn about Christ?

What are we to learn from Paul?

What must we, as children of the faith, receive in addition to encouragement?

Why did Paul issue warnings?

Why did Christ issue warnings?

What is implicit in these warnings?

What is characteristic of the life of man?

What is our understanding and reaction to Paul's teaching contained in the *wind of doctrine, sleight of men, cunning craftiness, whereby they lie in wait?*

What are the traits of false teachings?

Why does the Bible stress evil and evil teachings?

What is to be our reaction to false teachings being planned and organized?

What are the characteristics of false teachers?

How can we recognize false teachings?

What is to be our attitude toward false teaching?

What is the result of false teaching?

Why do we have apostles, prophets, evangelists, pastors and teachers?

Chapter 19

Growing Up Into Christ

> *But speaking the truth in love, may grow up into him in all things, which is the head, even Christ* [Eph. 4:15].

Why are we to grow in the truth of God's love?

What position is Christ to have?

What does *speaking the truth in love* mean?

What do people espouse regarding doctrine that is not in accord with the teachings contained in Scripture?

How has the phrase *speaking the truth in love* been interpreted?

What does the word *agape* mean as it is interpreted for *love*?

How is God's love seen as it pertains to us?

What further can be said about agape love?

What is *not* meant by the term *speaking the truth in love*?

How are we to hold *the truth in love*?

Why is there to be no question about the person of the Lord Jesus Christ?

Why is the church in her present condition today?

What is this love that Paul describes by saying, *But speaking the truth in love*?

Why does Paul use the term *My little children* in writing to the Galatians?

Chapter 20

Weaned from Milk

> *But speaking the truth in love, may grow up into him in all things, which is the head, even Christ:*
> *From whom the whole body fitly joined together and compacted* (knit together) *by that which every joint supplieth, according to the effectual* (effective) *working in the measure of every part* (each part doing its share), *maketh increase* (causes growth) *of the body unto the edifying of itself in love* [Eph. 4:15–16].

What is meant by *may grow up into him* (Christ) *in all things*?

What does Scripture continuously emphasize?

How does the truth of the Gospel grasp us as we continue to mature?

How are we to grow in Christ?

What is meant by Paul's statement, *Be not children in understanding; howbeit in malice be ye children, but in understanding be men*?

Why does Scripture consistently emphasize the importance of balance in the Christian life?

How does the truth of the Gospel grasp us?

What did Isaiah mean when he said, *Whom shall he teach knowledge? and whom shall he make to understand doctrine* (the message)? *them that are just weaned from the milk, and just drawn from the breast*?

What do Paul and Isaiah mean?

What do the piercing words, *yet they would not hear*, mean?

Why does Paul say that we should not be like children?

How does Paul both warn and praise the Romans?

How does the body have harmony and function in unison?

What enables the body to function?

What type of unity does Paul describe?

What does this have to do with unity in Christ?

How is this love seen in the Lord Jesus?

Chapter 21

Spirit Producing Fruit

> *But speaking the truth in love, may grow up into him in all things, which is the head, even Christ:*
> *From whom the whole body fitly joined together and compacted* (knit together) *by that which every joint supplieth, according to the effectual* (effective) *working in the measure of every part* (each part doing its share), *maketh increase* (causes growth) *of the body unto the edifying of itself in love* [Eph. 4:15–16].

How are we to face difficulties and examine them?

What brings unity unto being and what hinders it?

What is the true nature of the church?

What determines unity?

What truths are basic to having fellowship and unity with other people and with Christ?

With whom do we not have much in common?

What are we to believe?

With whom are we to have a right relationship?

What is the difference between activity and life in Christ?

What are the results of the blessings of the Spirit?

What really matters in a church?

What happens when there is a failure to understand the doctrines of the church?

What is the nature and character of our activities in the church?

What is our first task in light of the Gospel and the teachings of Christ?

What vital questions need to be asked regarding the church?

How are we to examine ourselves in the light of the Gospel?

What is the call of the New Testament?

What developments may occur after receiving the call to respond?

Bibliography

Barth, Markus. *Ephesians 1-3*. Garden City, NY: Doubleday, 1974.
Calvin, John. *Calvin's New Testament Commentaries*. Grand Rapids, MI: Eerdmans, 1973.
Calvin, John. *Calvin's Sermons on The Epistle to the Ephesians*. Carlisle, PA: Banner of Truth, 1973.
Calvin, John. *Institutes of the Christian Religion*. Philadelphia, PA: Westminster.
Lloyd-Jones, Martyn. *Christian Unity*. Grand Rapids, MI: Baker Book House, 1980.
Paxson, Ruth. *The Wealth, Walk and Warfare of the Christian*. London and Edinburgh: Oliphants, 1941.
Presbyterian Hymnal. Louisville, KY: Westminster John Knox, 1990.
Vine, W. E. *Vine's Expository Dictionary of New Testament Words*. McLean, VA: MacDonald.
Weber, Otto. *Foundations of Dogmatics*. Volumes 1 & 2. Grand Rapids, MI: Eerdmans, 1983

bibliography

Index of Scripture References
Volume Four

Job

25:4	16

Psalms

68:4–5	111
68:18	112, 113
68:18–19	112
143:2	15

Isaiah

28:9	167
28:10	168
28:11	168
28:12	168

Matthew

3:15–17	48–49
4:1	48
5:3–9	33
5:43–48	55
5:48	133
7:15	148
7:21	74, 75
11:27	76–77
12:43–45	44
16:24	76
16:28	76
23:23	148

Mark

1:11	76
5:6–9	44
8:23–25	67

Luke

2:36	118
4:1	48
22:29–30	58

John

1:11–14	128
1:16	128
2:1–2	57
3:3–5	186
3:4	138
3:7	138
3:16	157
4:10	128
4:12–14	128
6:44	25
6:63	49
8:44	103
9:2	66
9:6-7	66
12:49	48
13:13	74
13:13–14	81
13:34	157
14:1	71
14:6	161, 176
14:15	158

John - continued

14:16–17	51
14:21	157
14:23	105, 158
14:26	49
15:5	178, 181
15:10	159
15:26	51
16:8	52
16:13	49
17:11	104
17:21	155
17:26	157
18:36–37	58
20:19–23	50
20:22	51

Acts

1:4–8	49
2:4	50
2:38	94
4:12	79
9:1	147
9:3–4	147
9:5–6	147
9:6	147
10:44–48	52
16:14	92
17:21	144
17:28	104
17:30	24
19:1–2a	94
19:2b	94
19:3–5	94
20:28–29	148
20:29	143
20:31	148
20:31–32	143
21:9	118
26:16	118

Romans

1:16–17	85
1:17	86
1:18–25	24–25
3:20–23	85
3:24	86
4:5	86
4:9–12	87
5:1	54
5:8	157
5:10	54
6:5	93
6:11–18	38
7:4	38
8:6	54
8:15	56
8:17	40
8:26–27	35
8:26–30	57–58
8:30	25
8:34	57
10:5	37
10:8–9	85
11:33–34	99
12:10–13	75
12:14	55
13:10	159
14:17	54
16:17–18	168
16:19	169

1 Corinthians

1:12	41
1:13	94
1:30	131
3:16–17	59
6:9–11	45
6:11	45
6:19–20	27, 59
8:5–6	80
8:6	77
10:1–2	94

Scripture Index

10:15–17	39	5:19–23	177
10:17	37, 39	5:22–23	33, 60, 61, 158
12:3	78	5:22–26	30–31
12:4–7	109–110	6:10	14, 159
12:8–10	111		
12:11	110	**Ephesians**	
12:12	37		
12:12–13	41	1:1	102
12:13	58, 96	1:2	18
12:14	133	1:3	107
12:26–27	41	1:3–5	26
13:12	72	1:4	11, 19, 24
14:20	167	1:18–20	105
14:33	55	1:19	27
15:55	115	1:22–23	36
15:57–58	115	1:23	111
		2:1	25, 53, 105
2 Corinthians		2:4	158
		2:7	170
4:10	40	2:8–9	66
4:17–18	71	2:10	16, 19
5:10	14	2:13	27
5:17	14	2:13–17	123
5:21	15, 86	2:14	30, 54
10:17	81	2:16	36, 38, 39
12:8–12	63	2:18	55, 100, 176
12:9	74	2:19	103
		2:20	120
Galatians		2:21	11, 45, 135
		2:22	105
1:1	118	3:5	11
1:11–12	118	3:10	42
2:20	97	3:14	127
3:27	38, 96	3:16	19, 27, 72
3:28	38	3:16–20	4
4:4–5	101	3:17–19	127
4:5–7	56	3:18–19	100
4:12	163	3:19	158, 170
4:15	163	3:19–20	3
4:16	163	3:20	27
4:19	164	4:1	4, 17, 26, 65, 126, 188
5:15–16	56	4:1–3	1, 5, 184
5:19–21	60–61	4:2–3	28, 190

Ephesians - continued

4:3	65, 78, 82, 88, 169, 173
4:3–6	99
4:4	36, 43, 64, 65, 66, 72, 194, 198
4:4–6	2, 33, 34, 51, 98, 192, 196, 206
4:4–16	123
4:5	73, 82, 90, 92, 93, 97, 200, 202, 204
4:6	101, 102, 104, 105
4:7	102, 106, 114, 116, 134, 210
4:7–13	208
4:8	113
4:11	116, 153
4:11–12	114
4:12	36, 108, 170
4:12–13	102, 137
4:13	82, 83, 108, 109, 122, 124, 129, 131, 134, 135, 136, 153, 154, 166, 212, 214
4:14	108, 137, 146, 160, 218
4:14–16	103, 216
4:15	154, 157, 166, 220
4:15–16	165, 173, 222, 224
4:16	108, 166, 172
4:17	19
5:2	158
5:5	76
5:15	19
5:18–20	20
5:27	11
5:30	37
6:12	43

Philippians

1:6	76
1:27	22
2:5	115
2:5–11	77
2:9–11	74
2:11	74
2:12–13	105
3:2	148
3:7–10	68
3:10	40
3:12–14	62–63
3:13	68
3:14	67
3:15	70
3:18	149
3:19	153

Colossians

1:9–10	129
1:10	75
1:18	37
1:22	39
2:3	81
2:8	148
2:9	77
3:1–2	72
3:15	38
3:23–25	75

1 Thessalonians

1:1–3	14
3:12	157

2 Thessalonians

1:11	14
2:10–12	149

2 Timothy

1:7	142, 174
1:14	49
2:2	162
3:16–17	12
4:5	119
4:8	76

Titus

2:7–8	23
2:10	23
2:11–14	8
2:12–13	71
2:13	77

Hebrews

6:9–12	21
6:11	22
6:12	22
7:25	57
11:6	87
12:6	162

James

1:6	140–141

1 Peter

1:23	25
2:2	139
2:9	25
3:18	48, 99

2 Peter

1:4	103
2:1–2	149
3:18	16, 140

1 John

2:5–6	20
2:23	80
3:2	60, 72
3:3–5	10
3:20	62
3:21–24	62
4:8	158
5:3	159
5:12	80

2 John

1:6	159

www.ingramcontent.com/pod-product-compliance
Lightning Source LLC
Chambersburg PA
CBHW062013220426
43662CB00010B/1312